Parents play a far bigger role in the ... society would have us believe. The tragedy is that even as parents ... their children and desperately desire to see them walk with Christ, they may ... to realize that some of the very things they do to help them follow Christ may ultimately drive them away from the church and even Christ. *Going, Going, Gone!* is a must read for any parent who wants to see their young adult children succeed socially, academically, and spiritually when they graduate from high school!

—**Val Nordbye, Mom and National Director of Campus Ambassadors**

The information found in *Going, Going, Gone!* significantly improved my relationship with my teenage son. The change in me was so obvious that my son sent me a thank you letter during his freshman year of college. He thanked me for changing the way I approached him in high school and listed the changes that greatly impacted him. He credited the changes for being the reason he was walking with the Lord in college!"

—**Rick Rablin, Father and Senior Systems Analyst, Alaska Airlines**

Today it is clear that we are not connecting with many of our young people. *Going, Going, Gone!* is an insightful and challenging look at the reasons so many teens are distant from their parents and church! It will challenge you, alter your perspective, and change the course of your relationship with your teenager!

—**Tom Scott, COO Association of Christian Schools Intl.**

Anyone who lives or works with teenagers must read this book. Over 70 percent of young people make a departure from their faith after they graduate from high school. But parents and youth pastors can help change that if they act now, *before* their kids go off to college or work life. Jeff Schadt has spent thousands of hours interviewing and counseling students. In this book, he paints a vivid picture of how to approach teens using the discipleship model that Jesus employed. It's all in your Bible, but Jeff expertly directs the reader and overlays the context of today's youth culture. This provides guidance for shepherding our young people before they're gone.

—**Brian Raison, Author & Founder of *College101.org* and youth development educator at The Ohio State University**

University campuses can be very perplexing for freshmen. With freedoms to do what they want like never before, they need wisdom. How do we prepare them for such an onslaught of temptations and trials? Jeff Schadt's research into this culture will help guide you in guiding them. This is a book that needs to be in the hands of parents, youth pastors, and most importantly, youth themselves.

—**Dr. Darryl DelHousaye**
President of Phoenix Seminary

Going, Going, Gone!

Protecting Teens' Hearts That Are On The Edge

by Jeff Schadt

dawson**media**

DEDICATION

To my wife, Deedee Schadt,
and our children:
Heather, Jennifer, Paul, and Eric.
Whose willingness to genuinely sacrifice
for YTN enabled *Going, Going, Gone!*
to be synthesized in my heart and soul.
Apart from each of them and all they teach me
I would not be who I am today.
They are the treasure God brought into my life!

To my Mom
who did not give up on me in school
when some teachers did.
She too has sacrificed for YTN
and has been invaluable in assembling this book.
Her faithful prayers and belief in me
have been a tremendous blessing.

CONTENTS

FOREWORD

Josh McDowell

———

I had the opportunity to begin a friendship with Jeff Schadt when he, along with the National Network of Youth Ministries and Mission America Coalition, called a national strategy meeting on "the loss of youth from the church." At the conclusion of that meeting the group voted to form the Youth Transition Network and asked Jeff to head the effort.

In the summer of 2005, Jeff and I spent a half-day together in Texas discussing "the loss of youth from the church" and the Youth Transition Network. At the conclusion of that day, I am sure Jeff did not anticipate my response. I decided to issue him a challenge: "Jeff, after our time together I am convinced you are anointed for this purpose. The only question I have for you is, are you willing to go to the poor house for it?" Neither I nor Jeff knew how prophetic that statement would be as Jeff has sacrificed beyond many I know to pursue the dilemma confronting the church concerning our young people.

Since our meeting in Texas, Jeff and a small loyal team at YTN have worked to assemble a team of ministries to address the loss of youth and build a national transition website, LiveAbove.com, to connect high school seniors to college ministries before they leave home. They also have met with more than 1,500 students in small groups to begin to understand the students' perspectives regarding why so many teenagers exit the church.

The challenge of reaching and keeping our youth has been one of my top priorities for many years. In my book *The Last Christian Generation,* I addressed the need to reexamine the church's approach to young people. Over the last several years the urgency has only increased.

Today we are witnessing a growing trend of younger and younger students dropping out of their youth groups and churches. In fact, today many large youth groups will have just a handful of juniors and very few, if any, seniors.

Many factors impact our youth and their faith. After 50 years of working with young people, I have become convinced that parents are the key to raising up the next generation of godly men and women who will radically pursue the Lord. Our families in the church can either be the one safe haven for young people in a hostile world, or an environment that will discourage their faith. The youth culture, entertainment, and media undermine their Christian convictions every minute of every day. Sunday morning church and Wednesday evening youth group meetings in their present state are by themselves unable to counter the impact of our culture.

Parents and the family structure remain the best hope we have for raising up the next generation of believers. In saying this, we must also acknowledge that the expectations and pressures placed upon parents and their time by our society have never been greater. Yet if we continue on our present course the outcome is clear; we will lose the next generation!

Given the forces at work on our young people today, we must increase the priority of our day in and day out connection with our young people. When we lose our connection to our teenagers, we will lose the battle for their hearts and minds. If we are to avert the powerful influences impacting our young people, it is vital that parents' relationships with their children remain strong as youth move into their pre-teen and teen years.

To accomplish this, we need to understand our teens' perspective on life, including school, church, and home. Our teens' need for love, acceptance, guidance, and their growing desire for independence, are often at war with their parents. This may lead parents to believe that having a good relationship with their teen is impossible and thus look to a youth pastor or another adult to guide their teen in these challenging years.

Yet research indicates that 69 percent of teens want more involvement in their lives from their parents. Many parents might say, "Not my teen!" but our studies indicate that their desire for involvement is real. The type of involvement they are seeking and receiving is often different, which creates a wall that causes parents to believe they cannot be a vital part of their teen's life.

Jeff Schadt has spent time with 1,500 teens seeking to understand the forces that are dampening teens' response to faith, parents, and youth leaders. *Going, Going, Gone!* looks deeply into the perspective of teens, helping parents and youth leaders better relate to their life experience. Greater understanding enables us to examine the view we hold of our young people and the approach we take to leading them. Altering the approach has yielded amazing changes in the relationships between parents and teens who have participated in his "Shepherding for the Future" seminars.

In the fast-paced world in which we live, it is easy to lose sight of what matters most. Continuing on the course we are on today points toward an outcome not so dissimilar to that of Europe and its aging and dwindling church. We as parents and leaders must rethink how we will raise up the next generation of church leadership! The future of the church, our nation, and its ability to influence the world is at stake.

While this is a universal issue, the battle is won and lost one student, one parent, one family, and one youth group at a time.

Every parent and every youth leader want their high school graduates to succeed in their life and faith beyond high school! *Going, Going Gone!* will help you assess your approach to your teenagers and help establish a course that will build a relationship and foundation that will set your students up to succeed, just as Jesus set His disciples up to succeed as He prepared to exit their lives.

ACKNOWLEDGMENTS

The assembly of this book has spanned many years and interactions with many wonderful people who taught me a great deal. They deserve much of the credit.

I want to thank Laurie Maschner, a college student whose heartfelt honesty in a random video interview served as the centerpiece to YTN's *Be Prepared* DVD and *Be Prepared* Kit. The DVD and Kit have been used with tens of thousands of students across the country. At the end of the video interview, Laurie, you said to me in tears, "If this helps just one student avoid what happened to me it will all be worth it." Laurie, it has helped many more than one. Thank you!

I would also like to acknowledge the many students who have been open and honest in video interviews and small group discussions pertaining to their faith and reasons for leaving the church. Apart from their honesty I would never have been brought to a point where I could reexamine some of the preconceptions I had about teens and their reasons for leaving the church. Their input, interaction, and subsequent study helped me wrestle more with Scripture than my entire seminary degree.

The following people have my deep appreciation for their involvement in my life and their contributions to making this book a reality:

Paul Fleishman, President of the National Network of Youth Ministries, and Paul Cedar, President of Mission America, helped pull together the first group of ministry leaders to discuss the loss of youth and form YTN. Their help and support has been amazing.

Bill Tell, Senior Vice President and Chief of Staff of The Navigators, worked alongside me both personally and in building the team of college ministries who came together to make the transition site for high school seniors, LiveAbove.com, a reality. His encouragement, mentoring, and service on the Board of YTN has been a blessing.

Stephen and Diana Boatwright have blessed YTN by serving on the Board since its inception, helping guide me and watching out for YTN as we sought God's direction.

The YTN Team:
Holly Bodine joined YTN at the ideal time and was in many ways the glue that kept YTN running. She helped gather the data from our sessions with students and worked diligently alongside me in a crucial season. Greg Hardin joined YTN without pay to build the technology that drives YTN today. Apart from his long hours and call to the mission, we could not accomplish all we do with such a small team. Rick Burdett keeps me headed in the right direction and his willingness to sacrifice alongside me for the call of YTN has been inspiring. Chris Renzelman and John Decker deserve great honor for their genuine sacrifice and dedication to reaching more students.

Val Nordbye, National Director of Campus Ambassadors, has been a source of great encouragement to YTN and to me. She heads the most proactive college ministry in pursuing the loss of youth by training her staff to help churches prepare high school graduates in churches and lead sessions for parents based upon this book and our "Shepherding for the Future" Seminar for parents of teens.

Deedee Schadt is a wonderful ministry wife who sacrificed

joyfully to launch YTN. She has fully supported YTN and me in more ways than I could list.

Heather and Jennifer, our daughters, have given us grace as parents as we sought to alter the way we approach them based upon what we were learning in this process.

Cathy Schadt has made very real sacrifices to help move YTN forward and given endless hours helping me to revise the book.

Steve and Barbara Uhlman, supported the development of LiveAbove.com and the Be Prepared resources, which would have never come into existence without their support. Their involvement started the process of interviewing many students, which captured our hearts and moved us toward seeking student input regarding the loss of youth.

Paul Carlson's faithful advice and involvement helped move YTN beyond its initial vision and encouraged me to keep going and to write this book.

Bob Kawa has pushed YTN to become all it should be in the eyes of the Lord. His encouragement and faithfulness have helped in many ways!

Kent and Shelly Bunger's participation was central in the development of "Succeed," the national preparation event for juniors and seniors in high school; their advice has impacted me greatly.

Dr. Paul Wegner invested in me at a crucial time, not just as a professor at Phoenix Seminary, but as a friend who cared and a mentor who encouraged. He helped me learn that knowledge is only a small piece of fighting the good fight!

Josh McDowell, teaching at a Campus Crusade Christmas Conference in Philadelphia many years ago, led me to the Lord. Years later we met to discuss forming YTN; at the end of a meeting he said to me, "I am convinced you have been anointed for this purpose. The only question I have for you is: are you willing to go to the poor house for it?" His statement helped propel my wife and me to sacrifice in order to pursue developing YTN.

INTRODUCTION

The day seemed like any other as I drove to Phoenix Seminary. It was already beginning to get hot and it was only April. After picking up some materials at the seminary, I was off to Arizona State University to participate in a meeting for campus ministers. About twenty ministry leaders were in the room. One of the agenda items was discussing how the ministries could work together to reach more students during the first week of school that coming fall.

As I listened to the discussion, thoughts began to ricochet in my head. Numerous ideas were discussed related to how to reach nonbelievers during the first week but there was no mention of connecting with youth group or Young Life graduates. As the discussion continued, this fact began to stir something within me. Even though I had once been on staff with Campus Crusade for Christ, this exclusive focus on outreach seemed wrong!

After contemplating whether or not to say something, I pitched in, "This may be a difficult question to ask in this crowd, but how many lost sheep are on this campus?" Silence fell, then someone asked, "What do you mean?"

I replied, "I'm talking about all the students who come from churches and youth ministries to ASU and do not become involved in anything." A lively discussion ensued as they estimated between 8,000 and 13,000 students. This number left me nearly speechless.

Then I asked, "What are we doing to reach them?" The answer: nothing. As the silence in the room continued, it was clear that the Holy Spirit was convicting everyone present.

That morning began a six-month discovery process of meeting with campus ministry leaders across the state. Together we concluded that the ministries need to be in touch with students before they arrive on campus or it's often too late. At that time, the ministries had no way to identify Christian high school graduates when they arrived on campus. The leaders in Arizona had observed that if they did not meet with youth ministry graduates in their first few days on campus, they were likely gone—even if leaders called and stopped by their room several times later in the semester. Our graduates walk onto campus anonymous, with no support network or accountability, and often fall in the first days on campus, before classes even begin!

I had no idea as the ASU meeting ended that my family's life would be affected in many profound ways. A mere nine months later my wife and I sold our home to found a ministry to address the loss of youth in Arizona; it was called Ministry Edge. Just five months later, with the help of the National Network of Youth Ministries and Mission America, we hosted a national meeting on the loss of youth in Arizona where thirty-five leaders voted to form the Youth Transition Network (YTN). Eventually YTN and Ministry Edge merged into one entity. This resulted in a coalition of nearly fifty ministries discussing the issues and building a national transition site called LiveAbove.com. Today this website has 4,700 ministries on 3,000 campuses that are waiting for seniors to contact them before they arrive.

Heading YTN for the past six years has afforded me the privilege of interacting with ministry leaders from youth, college, and career ministries across the country. I've had the freedom to interact with more than 1,500 teens pertaining to the loss of youth, their faith, and the reasons they leave the church. These times with students encompass over 400 interviews on camera and twenty-five focus group discussions with high school and college students.

Along the way we heard the reasons why students were checked out and even numb. Over time we began to analyze their reasons for leaving. We discovered three main components to the loss of youth: the way we approach teens in high school related to their faith, the lack of preparation for graduates, and the lack of effort to connect them to ministries before they leave home. We seem to assume that we have given them all they need to succeed when they leave home and yet all the statistics, both Christian and secular, point to the fact that the majority are not ready to handle life beyond high school. Many do survive the transition apparently okay, but our time with college students raised questions about that assumption as well.

One evening we took a pilot video about the transition to a college ministry meeting with thirty-five students at ASU. The video was just talking heads; we had not edited in any of the action scenes, campus shots, or music. It was just one student talking after another for about thirteen minutes. As a result, we expected to get mixed reviews, but we wanted to see if the story line was accurate and connected with the student audience. When the video ended spontaneous applause broke out in the audience and it was not just polite applause, but heartfelt and lengthy.

We were shocked by this response and asked why they applauded. As the first girl started to share she broke down crying; a second girl started to share and she also broke down crying. Then a guy opened up and he too started to cry. The leaders of the ministry and I had no idea what was going on or what to do.

So I asked, "How many of you experienced something like this in your first weeks on campus; you were hurt but then found a ministry to be connected to?" More than two-thirds of the hands went up! What horrified us all that evening was that these were students we counted as staying with the faith! Their ministry leaders had no idea how many had been wounded so deeply in the transition. Their faith did not sustain them, they were not prepared for the change, and they were alone their first days on campus.

Going, Going, Gone! looks into many of these issues. It is my wife's and my prayer that this book will help parents and ministry leaders begin a process of reassessing the approach taken with their pre-teens and teens as they look to set them up to succeed on their own. Our time with students and ministry leaders has altered everything we are doing with our own pre-teens and teens, and we have seen great fruit from the changes.

CHAPTER ONE

GOING, GOING, GONE!

———⟨⟩———

*K*im's heart is beating quickly. It's her eighteenth birthday and she's heading home from high school with just one thing on her mind. Her parents are also excited to celebrate her birthday and are looking forward to seeing her graduate in just two months. To them everything is going well. Their son is in full-time ministry at their church and their daughter is doing fine. They're proud of her; she's a good student involved in her church youth group; she has not been the typical troublesome teen. They're thankful that she is not like so many in their church who have gone off track in high school.

Arriving home for a family celebration, Kim feels like she is about to explode. The sense of fear that has built up within her over the last couple of years threatens to overwhelm her. As she walks through the door, her parents greet her with smiles and hugs, unaware of the storm that is about to strike them with gale force winds.

Kim knows that her parents have no idea of what has really been going on in her life. She has managed to play the role expected of her for several years, acting as if she were on a stage. While her parents have sensed something has been changing with Kim, they have no idea the depth of the deception that has been taking place. Kim believed she was doing what was best for everyone, because she did not want to hurt them or destroy their reputation. It also made living with her parents trouble free. She was, after all, keeping the peace by not letting them know the things in which she was really involved.

Knowing that she is about leave what has been her home for the last eighteen years, Kim's mind races as her parents hug her. She scrambles for the words to say what will surely be a shocking revelation to her parents. Her course is set. It is a path that at this point no one, including her parents, will be able to dissuade her from taking. She has hidden her real life from them for nine months. It's time for the deception to come to an end.

As they sit down for their family celebration, Kim blurts out, "I'm moving out of the house tomorrow." Her parents, not believing what they have heard, raise their voices with a familiar, "What?" using a tone that cuts deeply. Their reaction only increases her determination not to listen to anything they have to say and to move out as quickly as possible.

In the ensuing discussion, Kim informs them that she will be moving in with a man who is six years older and that they can't stop her, because, after all, she is eighteen.

Later that night her parents lie stunned, wide awake in bed, pondering over and over, "How did this happen? How could we not know it was this bad? Where did she meet him? How long have they been seeing each other? This is a nightmare; this cannot actually be happening." Almost simultaneously they arrive at the stark realization that this is not a bad dream, and worse yet, they do not truly know their own daughter. Tears roll down their faces as they can only ask each other and God, "What went wrong? Our daughter is GONE!"

Speaking with students like Kim across the country, I'm struck by the discouragement and disillusionment I hear in their stories. From these discussions it is clear that students do not wake up one day and say, "I'm going to mess up my life today." Rather, their choices are part of a gradual process building for several years as their hearts drift ever so silently into the darkness, further and further from the Lord and their parents.

Kim is not alone. Based on research executed in the summer

of 2007 by LifeWay, 70 percent of eighteen to twenty-two year olds take a break from the church.[1] Every year 3.1 million high school students graduate in the United States.[2] About 31 percent, or 961,000, of these graduates attend church regularly.[3] If 70 percent leave the church, we have 673,000 walking away annually. Many do not move in with an older man, but the fact that they leave the church and enter lifestyles that often surprise and leave questions with their parents is undeniable. Many parents like Kim's do not see it coming. Kim's parents saw a teenager who seemed to have it together at home, at church, and academically. Therefore they believed all was well and that their child would do well when she left home.

Through our interaction with youth pastors across the nation it has become clear that the loss of youth begins before they leave home, during the junior and senior years of high school. Youth groups across the nation see a huge drop off in the attendance of juniors and seniors. As an example a youth group of eighty might have thirty freshmen, thirty sophomores, fifteen juniors, and five seniors. If students are checking out spiritually in high school, they're signaling an underlying problem that will contribute to the loss when they leave home and head into college or a career.

What makes this so alarming? When our teens leave home they are heading into what *USA Today* deemed the most dangerous year in the life of a teen. A headline article, "First Year of College is the Riskiest," chronicled data showing that accident, suicide, and alcohol-related death rates are the highest among recent high school graduates.[4] Later in this book, the "When They Graduate" chapter will discuss the forces that have a negative impact on students and lead to these statistics.

As parents and leaders we need to understand the real forces and points of stress that impact our high school students and graduates as opposed to counting on their return later in life. The LifeWay study that indicates a 70 percent loss of eighteen to twenty-two year olds from the church also concluded that less than 35 percent of those who leave return to the church by age thirty.[5]

If only 35 percent are returning every year, 438,000 young people beyond age thirty remain lost![6] In addition, it is likely that the percentage returning to the church will continue to decrease given the developing postmodern and accepting mindset among our youth. It is not wise to believe we can turn the tide on post-modernism among our youth with such a small percentage of believers in our nation and our diminishing influence in media and politics. To count on young people returning to the church would be to disavow what happened in Europe eighty years ago when postmodernism took hold. The young stopped returning, the church grayed and today, once full cathedrals and churches sit empty as museums. Some now serve as mosques.

When we count on young adults' return, we also overlook the challenges that the return often brings into the body. Today the divorce rate in the church is almost identical to that of the world, having risen dramatically over the past fifteen years.[7] Could the root of this fact be tied to the loss of youth issue?

When students leave the church and the roots of their faith in high school, they begin life on their own apart from the Lord. In these pivotal years they select their career, life style and often their spouse. Later, when family and marriage troubles arise, they frequently return to the church hoping that it will be the fix, yet the basis of their lives has not been built upon the foundation of the Lord. As a result, patterns of behavior have developed that are not easily broken. When the quick fix appears elusive, divorce is often the result. Ignoring the loss of youth problem contributes to many of the issues in the body of Christ. This has the world saying, "Look, they are no better than we are, so why listen to them?"

When I began hearing stories like Kim's and looking at the research, I started asking many questions:

- How could Kim keep her life secret from her parents while living in their home?
- Why are teens who grow up within the church so distant from God?
- Why do so many teens walk away from the church?
- Why doesn't our teaching impact the lives of our teens more fully?
- Who exactly are the lost according to Jesus?

As the head of the Youth Transition Network for the past five years, I have had the genuine privilege of interacting with young people around these and many more questions related to their faith and the reasons they are checking out at younger and younger ages. I am eternally grateful for the many students who have openly shared their lives, struggles, and failures, helping the YTN team to gain insights into the forces dampening their hearts' response to God.

Many of the reasons students gave for leaving the church first struck me as feeble, weak, or simply an excuse. Yet as we invested time interviewing both individuals and groups, many of their reasons began to make sense. They presented a picture that helped us explain why a child at age five can accept the Lord, ask genuine questions, and be excited about the Lord only to have, in their pre-teen and teen years, their hearts become distant and callous to the truth, their Lord, and often their parents.

We will examine these issues in chapters three through six and begin unpacking antidotes in chapters seven through eleven. But before exploring the insights gained from our teens, it is imperative that we examine the gap that exists between church leadership, parents, and our young people today. This will greatly impact our understanding and willingness to address the issues at hand.

CHAPTER TWO

BRIDGING THE GAP

—⊸⊸⊸—

*A*s John walks into the house his mom asks, "How was youth group tonight?"

"Good," he says, conveniently burying his head in the refrigerator to avoid eye contact. John's mom has become accustomed to one-word answers these past few years and attributes it to him being a teenager who is trying to become his own person.

That's why the next week, when John comes to her and asks, "Do I have to go to youth group?" she's surprised and a bit dismayed. When she asks why, John says, "I've heard this all before and my friends don't go anymore."

Thinking to herself that John will be leaving home soon and then she will not be able to make him go she says, "I would really like you to go. I won't make you, but you still need to come to church with us on Sunday."

John walks away pleased. He doesn't have to be involved in youth group anymore. He has become one more in a long list of students who leave their youth group in their junior or senior year of high school.

John's mother doesn't realize what she's done. By giving him permission to simply attend church but to skip youth group, she has helped him take the first step toward leaving church altogether. Although he may attend church with his parents, his friends are not there and the sense of genuine fellowship with the throngs of adults does not resonate. This is important because community is one of the more significant

factors postmodern young people use to evaluate their world.
The deeper issue is that the interaction between John and his mom
did not explore the real reasons why he was leaving the youth group.
He gave an answer that could be verified but was not truly driving his
choice. The gap between John and his mom in terms of understanding
is significant, and probably was missed by his mother altogether.

In many ways the gap between John and his mom is a chasm I have struggled with as well. When we first began talking with students to understand why they were leaving the church, the greatest challenge for us was getting out of the way. It was difficult for me to listen and truly understand teens' reasons for departing. My reaction kept me from digging deeply into typical answers like hypocrisy. I viewed that as an excuse because we are all hypocrites at some level.

As my time with students continued and similar answers kept surfacing, I realized that *I* was the problem, not the 300 youth with whom I had interacted. This was a very disturbing thought for a seminary-trained forty year old with four children. What I discovered in myself was a troubling sense that I knew the truth and they just needed to understand it. Actually my own understanding was blocked by a generational divide, a divide between a modern approach to life and truth and a more postmodern approach to the same.

I was forced to come to grips with how my predisposition from my church experience and generation created a gap of understanding. I had been looking for answers consistent with my thought process and beliefs, yet few if any of teens' reasons for leaving aligned with my predisposition. I was forced to go beyond my predisposition, which was based upon the decrease in biblical literacy. This pointed me toward a knowledge-based solution: teaching more doctrine, biblical worldview, and apologetics. Such answers had simple solutions that were more linear and far less challenging to my faith and my day-to-day walk with the Lord. These answers connect with some youth and greatly impact them and their faith. However, the percentage of those who respond to these answers seems to be decreasing as the postmodern mindset permeates an ever-increasing number of our youth. What can we do for those who seem immune to intellectual arguments for faith?

Speaking with Christian school administrators helped me move past my predispositions. Although teaching Bible, doctrine, worldview, and apologetics, these schools were still encountering an equal or sometimes even greater loss of students upon graduation. Only a small percentage of their junior and seniors I spoke with were still involved in a church youth group. And these students' reasons for leaving the church were virtually identical to those of public school students who attended youth groups.

Many of us have heard or read about the gap between modern and postmodern thinking. There are even debates about what these terms mean. In spite of these differences it is clear from our time with students that we as older adults approach life and process information very differently. I find that, like me, many leaders today have the same desire to argue against a postmodern thought process, to try to convince students that the way they think and how they approach life is wrong. We may win that argument with some, but how many? This is one of my greatest concerns for the church and our young people.

I find it interesting that we want to teach students to approach church, faith, and Scripture the same way we do when it has been on our generation's watch that our nation has moved further and further away from God. Although we have lost much of our influence in the world, the media, and even in politics, in spite of massive expenditures, we still believe we know best and that our youth should approach the faith exactly as we have. There was a similar response to postmodern thinking in Europe eighty years ago. The result? The church in Europe shriveled to a mere skin of its once vibrant self. Am I arguing for the emergent church? No, I am questioning continuing as we have for all these many years.

Coming to grips with this reality resulted in a study examining how Jesus approached the culture in Rome as well as the approach He took to shepherding His disciples. It is clear that Jesus was not working with modern thinkers such as ourselves, but rather pre-modern thinkers. Signs and wonders like miracles, healings, and the casting out of demons were important to these people. They provided the tangible evidence needed to validate the reality of the truth Jesus was teaching. Around the globe today, the gospel goes out to pre-modern people groups. Here, we still find frequent reports of miracles occurring among them.

The gospel for us as moderns has been much more an exercise of proof, evidence, apologetics, and worldview rather than reliance upon signs and wonders because that is fundamentally how we evaluate reality. Yet our young people today are in some ways more like the pre-moderns. They seek community, authenticity, and an experience in the community that validates the truth we are teaching.

Having come to a better understanding of our young peoples' issues and perspective, their bent toward experience no longer concerns me. In fact it is an incredible opportunity similar to what Christ found in the culture of His day. There is great potential for the truth to take root deeply in the hearts of our young people when we understand their issues and how to connect with their mindset.

Paul understood the need to alter his approach for different audiences; his approach in the synagogues and with the Gentiles was often quite different. In Athens, according to Acts 17:23, he saw the inscription to an unknown god. Then in 1 Cor. 9:22, he explained, "I have become all things to all men, that I may by all means save some." We as leaders today face this challenge, not just with unbelievers, but with those who have grown up within our churches and are now evaluating their faith differently than ourselves.

Having come to appreciate our youth, I find great hope. If we alter our approach, this generation may accomplish more for the kingdom than the combination of all the modern generations which have seen our country slide further and further from the Lord in spite of our high view of truth and our desire to hold a moral line. We see great hope that, given a desire and willingness to reconsider our approach to youth, we will see the trend reversed in our country.

Hope is defined as:
1. A feeling that something desirable is likely to happen
2. A chance that something desirable will happen or be possible
3. Somebody or something that seems likely to bring success or relief[8]

From where comes our hope at YTN for reversing this loss? It springs from the next generation's need for authentic community. The next generation of teens could be far better at reaching America than recent generations have been. We modern mindset thinkers become concerned with an emphasis on experience because this is not consistent with our inherent understanding of what matters. As a result, we frequently overlook the lack of community and authenticity in our churches and cling to the truth *we* believe in. The next generation desires a change in the culture of our churches. They desire an experience more consistent with the truth we teach them. If we can keep them, they could bring a new emphasis that would be beneficial to our ministries.

Look at the book of Acts and the first century church where the writer talks about "their numbers being added to daily." This was happening because they were "devoted to the apostles' teaching" as well as a long list of community-based factors that provided an amazing experience for the pre-modern thinkers of the day. We moderns tend to minimize or become fearful of *experience* because we place the priority on truth alone or because our experience in the body has been difficult. The next generation will not overlook the value of community and the impact positive experiences can have in reaching others.

We have been testing approaches including content that seeks to address the current issues of youth groups. When we approach our young people as valued believers and help them process why they are sensing that the "yoke is heavy and the burden is unmanageable," instead of the "yoke being easy and the burden being light," we have seen their hearts reignite for the Lord in a surprisingly short period of time.

If we pastors, parents, and leaders take the time to rethink our approach to our teens and take seriously their issues while providing our youth with ministries that have healthy communities, we will see our young people quickly become far more devoted to the biblical teaching that means so much to us. In so doing, we will raise up the next generation of leaders who will lead a church with a more vibrant community. This can result in throngs of new believers being added to our numbers daily because the church will remain devoted to "the apostles' teaching" and provide an experience that is dynamic, alive and consistent with the truth we teach.

It takes only one generation to turn the world upside down. God can do amazing things, and often He chooses to do it through youth. Remember Martin Luther, John Calvin, and the apostle John? If we, God's people, will humble ourselves and pray and seek His face and turn from our ways, He will forgive us and heal our land, and our children in the process. Or even better, our children may be the process as God helps us bridge this generational gap.

QUESTIONS AND REFLECTIONS

Reflection

Jesus entered a Roman culture much like our own. It was the most sophisticated and educated culture of its time. The Empire had become fixated on pleasure and entertainment where: massive banquets/parties went to excess, plays included the execution of actual prisoners, and the gladiator games saw men killed for entertainment. Many unwanted births were handled by exposing infants to the elements in countryside. The government of Rome was passing laws requiring higher taxes upon Romans with dual incomes to restore a focus on family.

Jesus could have entered this culture focused on its many evils, railing against them. Is that what we find in His ministry? It is clear that Jesus trained His disciples to love the unlovable through actual interactions with people like the Samaritan woman, leper, prostitute, and the hungry crowd.

Questions for parents and leaders:

How has our culture and mindset shaped our approach to the young people we shepherd?

How do you think Jesus would approach our post-modern generation?

How might we alter our approach to reach and encourage our young people to continue in their faith today?

CHAPTER THREE

UNDERSTANDING THEIR ISSUES

*I*t was Saturday and YTN was holding its first session related to the loss of youth with a group of about sixty juniors and seniors at the Arizona State Youth Convention. We had prayed for weeks that the students would be honest, transparent, and help us understand the issues that had so many young people leaving the church.

The session had a twofold purpose; to roll out a preparation session for students and to incorporate a research component. After sharing honestly about the trials of recent years in my life, we began the research component by breaking into small groups. Students were asked to discuss why they believed so many youth were leaving the church. Then each group reported back their compiled reasons while a student recorded them on a white board.

It took about twenty minutes for each of the nine small groups to come up with ten reasons why they believed so many of their peers were leaving the church. Our fear that they would not be open and honest was shattered with the third reason given: sex. To say I was taken aback is an understatement. I had not even remotely expected sex to come up as a reason for leaving the church.

I responded, "Okay, you surprised me with that one and I'm confused. Why would sex make you want to leave the church?"

Both the young man who had shared the reason and the group became silent; the whole room took on a weighty feeling.

I asked, "Is the reason sex makes you want to leave the church *because you want to have sex and you know you can't as part of the church?" A swift and decisive "No!" came from all corners of the room.*

So I responded, "Well then, why?" The boy who had listed the reason finally blurted out from the awkward silence, "Because we have had sex!" As I scanned the room about two-thirds of the heads in the room were nodding in agreement, again setting me back on my heels.

I probed. "Okay, so you've had sex. Why does that make you want to leave?" They answered, "Because we feel so guilty." I pressed on. "Why does guilt make you want to leave the church?"

They answered in rapid-fire responses:

"It makes us not want to come on Sunday."

"It makes us not want to open the Bible."

"It makes us want to run and hide because we're going to hear more of what we need to live up to and we're already failing!"

Then I asked, "Do you have anyone you can share that guilt with?" "No!" "What about your parents?" The whole room exploded with energy. "No way!"

"They would take away my car."

"They would not let me see my boyfriend or girlfriend again."

"They would ground me for life."

"They would kill me!"

"Well, can you share it with your youth workers?" They again said no and when I asked why not, they told me, "Things leak, parents find out and you become labeled as the problem kid in the church."

Altogether this first exercise yielded thirty-six reasons why teens were leaving the church. In one of the early sessions with students, I had dismissed some of their responses as invalid or excuses. Yet as we conducted more sessions and compiled the responses, we began to explore a number of what appeared to be highly charged reasons for students' leaving the church. In tracking the frequency of the responses across the country, nine reasons have shown up in every one of the twenty-five groups of teens who completed this exercise.

- **Bored**
- **Judgmental**
- **Guilt**
- **Parents' Faith**
- **Not addressing my real needs**
- **Fun and games**
- **Hypocrisy**
- **Not valued**
- **Pressure in my group**

Later in this chapter we'll look at each of these reasons through the eyes of our young people.

But first let's step back and look at what we discovered from analyzing the list of reasons we received. When we categorized the responses into individual faith and community reasons, the picture was so one-sided it was shocking. Seventy-five percent of the reasons for leaving fell into the community category. This was striking to us because when we're participating in youth events and speaking in churches around the country, we're most often asked to teach on issues that target individual faith.

Let's categorize the nine reasons that have come up in every session.

- **Bored**   A community reason
- **Judgmental**   A community reason
- **Guilt**   Both an individual and
                                              community reason

- **Parents' Faith**   A community reason
- **Not addressing my**   A community reason
  real needs

- **Fun and Games**   **A community reason**
- **Hypocrisy**   **A community reason**
- **Not valued**   **A community reason**
- **Pressure in my group**   **A community reason**

In youth work today we spend a vast majority of time addressing teens' individual faith, including their knowledge and purity. Yet the reasons they give for leaving the church weigh more heavily on the community side of ministry. A major disconnect is apparent. We as modern thinkers run many of our youth ministries and conduct the teaching. Even the more postmodern youth leaders came up through modern churches and seminaries. As modern thinkers, we're more individualistic and focused on knowledge of the truth. This next generation values community and experience and looks to these factors to validate the truth. This is comparable to those whom Jesus sought to reach.

When we overlook the culture and community of our ministries, instead teaching almost exclusively about individual faith and holiness, we are not using significant segments of Scripture that address the function of a healthy body of Christ. Such teaching might help counteract what our students are saying about their community and its impact upon their desire to stay involved with their youth group, church, and personal faith.

Stop and think about the last ten messages you heard or gave. What percent targeted some facet of individual faith and holiness versus the community of the body of which you are a part? We inherently focus on individual faith when our students are looking at the culture of their ministries. They may think, "good lesson," but when they look to their youth ministry culture and community and see clearly that it isn't working, they question why they should stay.

Our sessions with teens raise the question as to whether we as modern leaders have been looking for solutions consistent with our mindset and approach rather than understanding what it will take to become all things to all people, including our own youth.

Examining the Reasons Given for Leaving

Let's unpack some of the key reasons students have given for leaving the church or their faith.

Bored

The first time I heard this I thought it would be based upon teens not having enough fun, games, or video game consoles in their youth room like they may have seen at some of the more cool churches. But instead the teens were referring to the repetitive nature of the teaching. Let me ask a question: Do you think the disciples or the masses would say that they were bored with Jesus' teaching?

We heard from students, "We've heard this all before." Rarely are students hearing messages that move beyond faith, holiness or outreach. This seems to be driven by parents' and youth leaders' fear of teen failure. Concerned that our youth will get into drugs, alcohol, and sex, we focus on their individual faith being strong enough to withstand these temptations so that they can live a holy life and reach their friends. We may use different passages or examples from the Scriptures but the message is often the same. If they have grown up in the church, they may have heard many of the examples ten or more times as well.

If we are boring our young people with messages about an all powerful, unending God we should be ashamed. How does this compare with the Lord who, during His ministry, had to retreat from throngs of people who were clamoring to hear more?

Part of teens' boredom also arises from what they call lack of connection. Connection stems from two distinct areas, purpose and need. We hear consistently that "the youth group or Christian school does not address my real needs." This often refers to the nature of the community along with issues they are facing at home or school. Second, it refers to the purpose of their youth group. Students do not sense much of a purpose outside of keeping them from failing. Combined, these factors lead to boredom and a "go ahead, try to surprise me with your teaching" attitude, which often drives us to be more creative, but does not target the underlying problems.

Fun and Games

We've been surprised by the consistency of this issue which seems to be driven by the age and perceived maturity disparity in youth groups. In interacting with juniors and seniors, we often hear that they're sick of the drama and fun and games. Juniors and seniors report that the games are goofy, immature, and they no longer want to be part of them. Part of this difference is driven by the fact that juniors and seniors are more self-conscious about how they look, male-female relationships, and how they are perceived.

We've heard from young ladies that the drama related to relationships—the "who likes whom" and "what happened between so and so"—among the underclassmen is another reason why upperclassmen tire of the youth group community.

Judgmental

This is typically understood by adults to mean that the church and adult population are too judgmental of teens' behavior and *sin* in general. Our discussions led us to realize that it has much more to do with the culture of their youth ministry. Frequently this is mentioned in relationship with how quickly some of their peers judge them related to who they are, what they say and do, and how they look. It also refers to the way mistakes and failures are handled within the youth group. They perceive that in their community at church and also at home, failure will result in judgment rather than encouragement and help. This directly ties to why they feel the youth group does not meet their real needs. Gossip and leaks pervade the culture, resulting in a breakdown of trust and true community.

Not Valued

Our students frequently do not feel valued by or valuable to the church. They perceive that they are to be present, but not heard. They also sense they are not trusted in the context of the church and Christian school.

After an event where we had some students and ministry leaders addressing the loss of youth, we debriefed with the students by asking what they thought of the time. The response was shocking. One young man asked if we wanted to hear what he really thought. Once assured, he said, "This is the first time I have ever heard or sensed that young people are truly important and valued by ministry leaders." As I reflected upon his comment I had to admit that I rarely deliver such messages or hear them communicated from church and ministry leadership. We must clearly communicate that our young people are important and valuable and that we want to hear from them. We must also listen and implement at least a portion of what they bring forward.

This issue is not confined within the church. In April 2009, Ohio State University hosted a "Leadership for Tomorrow" conference. In the final session, a youth panel discussion featured six student leaders, each active with a variety of organizations, social action, or environmental projects. These current college leaders spoke directly to the issue of adult/youth interaction.

> *"Our experiences mean a lot. We've done a lot. We have hidden experiences, but our age is seen as inexperienced. We know we need to gain trust. But we hate being talked down to."*

"We need adult leaders to boost confidence. We need mentors! But kids are afraid to ask adults to be a mentor."

"Give kids the opportunity to lead. Provide an atmosphere for student involvement. Then leaders must make the opportunity to help new leaders emerge."

Our challenge is to listen, hear, and then coach this tremendous energy and keep our young people engaged.

Parents' Faith

This reason for leaving the faith comes up in every session and is typically echoed by numerous students in each group. It appears that there are three primary reasons they perceive faith to be their parents' and not their own. First, some students feel the faith has been forced upon them by their family. Second, is how their parents live out their faith at home. Third, is whether or not students felt the freedom to question the faith or were challenged and extended the freedom to make the faith their own.

Some students feel that they have never been given a choice related to their faith by their parents. Parents who rarely talk about their faith and their struggles, or go through the faith motions in a routine way are more likely to have students who say that what they believe is actually their parents' faith. This stems from the fact that their own faith does not seem genuine or life changing. Both are vital for youth today given that their generation seeks authenticity and experience from their faith. Students indicate that their parents believe in the Lord but the students themselves are not sure if they believe what they have been taught.

Students who did not feel the freedom to question their faith, especially with their parents, have not perceived the freedom they needed to internalize the knowledge they have been taught. Frequently, those who have grown up in the church make professions of faith at young ages. They begin life in Christ with a simple childlike faith. As they get older these same students develop analytical skills that are naturally put to use in every area of their lives, including their faith. Often parents expect the church to challenge students on faith issues, but the culture of our ministries rarely encourages wrestling with what they have been taught as truth since a young age. Many times these questions are perceived as doubts, not just part of growing up, which quickly stifles real discussion. As a result, students quickly perceive that questions equal doubts. Given the expectations they perceive growing up in the church, students believe they should never struggle in their faith. They stop asking questions, though the questions still silently linger.

The approach and culture of our families and ministries will either seek to recognize these growing cognitive abilities and see them as an opportunity, or will approach them like, "You know this and you should believe it."

The other day my daughter and I were driving home from her high school orchestra concert. She asked, "Dad, do you ever have doubts about whether God is real?"

Instead of saying no and trying to convince her of God's existence, I asked, "Why? Do you have doubts?"

She said yes. I said to her, "Today I have no doubts about whether God exists, but I do have many questions I would like to ask him."

"Like what?" she asked.

"I'd like to ask God why it has been so hard to get the national ministries to truly commit to addressing the loss of youth and why He has asked us to make such significant financial sacrifices to pursue the call He gave us?" She had some of the same questions.

I continued, "At your age I had many doubts about whether God existed. I wondered if I was just praying to a wall." I told her that such questions are not necessarily doubts, but naturally occur as the brain matures and learns to analyze. We talked a while and I told her I was glad she asked the question and that she could ask me any question she wanted about life and faith. I did tell her that I wanted her to live her life like she believed as she got older and went off to live on her own, but that would be her choice. I also told her that the Lord loves children and says to have a childlike faith and that the Lord will be part of her life forever as a result of her childhood profession of faith!

Not Addressing My Real Needs

Needs vary from student to student. This raises the bar of complexity for any youth ministry. As we look at Jesus' ministry we see Him meeting the needs of individuals in the community. I would venture to guess He did the same for His disciples. As we began to understand the varying practical needs of high school students and the many things they felt unprepared for upon graduation, it became apparent that very little has been done to target those needs. An Ohio State University study conducted by Brian Raison concluded that a vast majority of students receive little or no preparation for the changes they will encounter following high school graduation. This fact contributes to the 26 percent drop-out rate of college freshman nationally.[9] Our underlying observation is that we often do not view youth ministry holistically.

Many churches approach reaching the inner city or taking missions trips in a holistic manner. In those contexts we often immediately consider how to meet the practical needs of people in order to give the gospel a platform in their lives. Yet when we return home, we seem to lose the radar for practical needs, perhaps because they are not as blatantly apparent. We find that youth ministries return from more holistic outreaches back to their building where everything will be approached with the exclusive model of teaching the truth.

Young people who are getting ready to head out on their own have a wide range of practical questions and needs. If we in the church viewed these needs holistically, we would also likely see that it would be better for the church and teens' parents to meet these needs rather than another source such as their schools or friends.

Some students in our groups are looking for jobs for the first time and others have no idea what they are good at or what they want to do with their lives. What if we helped them get ready to interview, to write a resume, to understand their personality type and how that affects their career choice? What if, in this process, as they began to understand how God wired them and the potential careers that might fulfill them, we also connected them with people in the church who had those jobs? They could come to understand those career paths and what they need to do to get into the field and what it takes to be successful. Might this give the gospel more credibility in their eyes because they are being helped with real needs? Would the time with adults who have the careers help them see that smart successful adults around them have a real faith and daily depend upon the Lord?

Holistic ministry is complex and requires more work but the outcomes would be powerful. Even Jesus assigned His disciples different parts of the practical effort of getting around and conducting ministry, trusting His still-maturing disciples with the money, travel, and food. When He left them, they already understood how to plan for their needs, manage their money, and handle life apart from Him. Many college students stumble because they are not ready to set priorities or manage their time and money when they leave home.

Guilt

This is far more pervasive than we expected, given the nonchalant manner in which many youth in our ministries carry themselves.

In sessions with teens, I frequently ask for a show of hands from those who feel like they have failed. Absolutely every hand goes up. Then I ask, "How many of you have failed big time?" Often two-thirds to three-quarters of the hands go up.

We have found that many rarely feel successful in their faith and far too many are carrying around a truckload of guilt that has no tailgate to drop the load. In the midst of all we have taught them, they have not learned how to handle their failure and resulting guilt. The culture of our ministries often discourages students from addressing their guilt with peers, leaders, or their parents. Left alone in their battle with guilt, they want to leave their church and youth group and avoid reading their Bible. Could this, rather than the fact that we are not teaching enough truth, be one of the reasons for the drop in biblical literacy? Are students tuning our teaching out and therefore not learning because they're buried in guilt and cannot listen to more that indicates they do not measure up? Much truth is being taught in youth groups and at youth events, yet students still appear to be checking out. Yes, there are places where truth is not taught, but at major youth events and in many youth groups the truth is held high. Yet students still leave the faith.

Because many students believe failure is not acceptable within the church, they will work together to hide failure from leadership and parents. This culture isolates them from the love, grace, and encouragement that could help them rise above failure and keep moving forward in their faith.

In the world we often hear that we learn more from our failures than our successes. Our students are hearing a message that says never fail—and if you do, cover it up. God took me through a period of successive failures to make me look deeply into this topic in Scripture. God does not see our failures as we do. Instead, He wants us to learn from them. He's there to pick us up in His loving arms and get us going again.

Hypocrisy

This reason for leaving could easily be used as a smoke screen, yet in our many discussions with teens it became clear that this is an issue we cannot afford to ignore. In our first sessions when hypocrisy was given as reason for leaving the church, youth were ho-hum when asked if the hypocrisy they were referring to dealt with leaders or adults in the church. This perplexed us until we asked, "Are you talking about hypocrisy within your youth group?" An immediate murmur of "Oh yeah" came from every corner of the room. The energy level in the room surged and the discussion that followed led us to dig more deeply into this issue.

In that session, together with the students, we defined hypocrisy in a youth group as leading an "intentionally deceptive dual life." To the students this meant knowing what to say to keep peace at home and how to act in church, while leading a very different life when away from these audiences. This was not a dual life characterized by blind spots, but one often deliberately contrived through planning and the assistance of other students within the youth group. We found that it was common for students to work together to get around the rules and to cover up their joint participation in the real (church) activities in which they were involved.

After identifying the intentionally deceptive dual life, we began asking students to estimate the percent of students who were leading this type of lifestyle in their group. We routinely heard numbers between 75 and 95 percent. We would place the typical range for the dual life between 40 and 80 percent.[10] In general, we found that the larger, more dynamic youth groups tended to have a higher percent estimated by their students than smaller youth programs.

In subsequent videotaped interviews with students involved in youth groups, we have documented numerous students who quit attending their church and had no desire to go back because every time they returned to their youth group they were sucked back into activities that made them feel worse about themselves and their faith. They decided the best option was to quit attending the church and never return.

If the dual life percentage in a group is above 50 percent, imagine how difficult it would be as a freshmen to enter the group seeking to fit in. It would be close to impossible to stand tall in the face of being invited to parties, being offered drugs, or being asked to hook up by a large percentage of the older more mature students in your group. This recipe for failure and the resulting guilt is dampening students' hearts to the truth we are teaching them, significantly impacting their biblical literacy.

Pressure in My Ministry

Stemming from the dual life research, we've had many students report that the pressure to have sex in their youth group and Christian school is higher than in the public high school. Finding this hard to believe, we asked, "How do you know and why is it higher?" They said it was easy to explain and understand. "At public high school everyone assumes you're having sex, so it is rarely if ever discussed. At our Christian high school everyone wants to know if you have had sex yet." They said that those who have become sexually active are seen as more "in the know" than those who have not and are often sought after and looked up to.

At one Christian high school where we videotaped students, a couple came up to us afterward and asked if they should get married. These two high school seniors believed that all 100 of their fellow senior classmates had experienced sex. While this may not have been accurate, it was clear that a vast majority had. In fact, the sex issue on campus was so great that at the beginning of their senior year they only knew of three other couples who had not had sex. The pressure was so significant that these

four couples made a pact together to be virgins when they gradu-
ated. By the time we interviewed them, nearing their graduation,
this one pair was the only couple who had not succumbed to the
pressure and temptation. They thought they should get married
because they did not have the support to hold out much longer.

When the peer pressure within our ministries goes against
what we're teaching, we face a losing battle with a generation
that values community and experience as much as the truth. Let
me say that again. When the peer pressure within our ministries
goes against what we are teaching, we face a losing battle with
a generation that values *community and experience* as much as
the *truth*. In discussions with students about the intentionally
deceptive dual life and their faith, it became clear that they had
earnestly tried to live out their faith at some point only to find
that it seemed impossible to live up to the varied expectations of
parents, ministry leaders, and friends. We must help our young
people rectify this situation.

THE YOKE IS HEAVY

When Gary called to tell me he had decided not to re-enlist in the Navy after his four-year hitch and was coming home, I was both excited and cautious. I had been discipling Gary since he was a high school sophomore. Now eight years later he would be home and our discipleship relationship could resume in earnest. The caution in my heart came from the extended periods of silence that had occurred over the past four years when he had fallen into significant temptation and squalor on deployment. He didn't think I was aware of this, but it had been easy to read between the lines in our sporadic conversations.

When Gary arrived back in town, he stopped by and our relationship picked up where it had left off. As we met to talk about spiritual things, he had many questions. He also found himself falling into old patterns developed on board ship in foreign ports of call. I will never forget the day Gary and I sat in the Sesame Inn for lunch; his questions were deep and disconcerting. Soon a question came welling up from deep within my heart. Was Gary truly a believer?

Years earlier following a Young Life summer camp, Gary shared with me that he had accepted Christ. We celebrated that and moved from an evangelistic to a discipleship relationship. It was an up and down time with Gary largely due to the challenges in his home environment. Now, sitting at a quiet table in a side room answering his questions, I thought there might have been another reason for the seesaw in his spiritual life.

As lunch ended and we stepped into his truck, our discussion continued. Then Gary fell amazingly quiet. I pondered, "Is it ever right to question someone's salvation?" Until this point it never seemed a place I should venture, being a mere man. But the nagging within my soul would not relent as the Holy Spirit prompted me to say something. In the midst of the silence, I simply asked Gary, "Are you sure you accepted Christ?" I braced myself for an offended response, only to be shocked when he broke down crying. His sobs became so deep as he drove that I felt I needed to grab the steering wheel. We pulled into a parking lot.

Once calmed down Gary said, "No, I am not a Christian." He proceeded to tell me what had happened at the Young Life summer camp. Gary had gone to the camp with his girlfriend; during camp she had broken up with him. He was distraught as he talked with one of the leaders, who took this as a great time to share the gospel. Gary heard little of what was actually said, but tuned back in as the counselor asked him if he would like to pray. At the conclusion of the prayer Gary knew this was not the prayer he had expected in this challenging time. He also knew he had not made a decision to accept Christ. To his surprise the counselor asked no follow-up questions; he just said "Great," and the day went on.

That night the camp director asked everyone who had received Christ that day to stand. A number of students stood throughout the auditorium. Gary did not. At that point the leader who had prayed with him prompted, "Gary, you accepted Christ today, stand up." In front of the eyes and expectations of many, Gary faced a choice: should he stand up and please these people, or should he say no?

Gary stood and was greeted with applause and congratulations. He went along with the lie. Returning home to tell me, he was once again greeted with joy, something he desperately needed because of his home life.

When I began to lay out how to live the Christian life, he chose to attempt to rise to my expectations because I loved and cared for him;

he didn't want to let me down. When Gary left for the military he was no longer under my care and no longer getting a dose of expectations on a regular basis. His so-called Christian life unraveled. Now eight years later Gary was in tears admitting, "I'm not a Christian. I've been living a lie all these years, living up to what people expected of me, but hollow inside."

Today many across the country are saying that we do not expect enough from teens. This concerns me because time and time again I have seen that expectations leaders place upon students tend not to lead to long-term fruit. This stems from teens' desire for validation, attention, and love. When we truly meet these needs, students will often do anything to try and meet our expectations.

Through our discussions with students who have left the church we repeatedly find that when that leader is no longer a part of their lives, neither are those expectations. Their Christian lifestyle and apparent growth often vanish. In short, teens met the expectations while they were with their leaders, but unlike Jesus' ministry with His disciples, when those leaders departed, so did all the performance that met their expectations. The activities were not being done to serve a wonderful, loving, and gracious God but rather to meet the perceived expectations of their leaders.

My wife and I first came to understand the challenge of expectations through a college ministry we led for a year and a half at a local church. Our students came mostly on Sundays, but many came to our men's and women's small groups on Wednesday nights, as well as to the social activities. However, it was obvious that most of these college students were not living a godly life when apart from us.

The students were very well versed in the Bible; many had gone to Christian high schools and had answers to almost every study and angle brought their way. They liked Deedee and me and all we did to serve them, but the truth was not making a difference in their lives. Having been on staff with Campus Crusade and seen disciples head off to full-time Christian work, we were amazed that we were not seeing more fruit.

Our frustration was on a slow boil for some time. We kept asking ourselves, "Why are they not growing?" We had been taught that if you are praying for them, meeting one-on-one with them, teaching them the truth and they are bringing some of their sin into the light (which many were), you should see some signs of life and change. However, none was apparent after eighteen months of our investment in their lives.

The group's obvious hypocrisy led to our own crisis of faith. We had no idea that our frustration and longing for genuine growth in our students would lead to a Sunday morning that would begin a fifteen-year journey toward addressing the loss of youth.

As we opened the Bible that Sunday morning, something needed to be said or done. We could not just continue teaching more truth and yet not see growth as individuals and as a group. So in the middle of our study that morning, I stopped and asked the students, "Why do you come?"[11] The question surprised them. I asked again, "Why do you come to church and our Bible studies? You're here, but we know how you live your lives and there appears to be a complete disconnect. So why bother coming?"

My honesty surprised them, but they couldn't deny the truth of my question. None of them could really give a good answer for why they came other than because they liked us. The fact is they would have kept coming every week with another leader and living a life that looked completely worldly the rest of the week as well. Some were coming because they were still living at home, others because their friend was, and others because it was the only place where they were plugged into a group their own age.

That Sunday opened the door to thinking outside of the box

about what we had been taught related to spiritual growth. It began a search to unlock the mystery of the students sitting in front of us. What I was not aware of that day was that this search would also help move me from the plateau I had reached in my own growth and willingness to take great risks for the Lord.

That Sunday morning led Deedee and me back to a study we had begun years before while on staff with Campus Crusade for Christ. The study examined how Jesus took twelve not-so-extraordinary young men and changed the world through them. The study was based on the assessment of our ministry, the lives of our disciples, and the plateau reached in our own walks with the Lord. It had revealed some very practical concepts that resulted in tremendous fruit in the lives of our disciples while on staff. The Lord spent a great deal of time with the disciples traveling from town to town, hanging out at campfires, foraging for food, and simply living life together. Jesus didn't spend the majority of His time with them in lecture; He frequently taught the disciples through life **experience**, **discussion**, and **questions**, forcing them to grapple with their beliefs, understanding, and faith.

Let's look at each of these based on specific Scripture:

Through Life Experience

In John 6:5-6 we find the account of Jesus feeding the five thousand.

> *Jesus therefore lifting up His eyes, and seeing that great multitude was coming to Him, said to Philip, "Where are we to buy bread, that these may eat?" And this He was saying to test him; for He Himself knew what He was intending to do.*

Jesus used this real life opportunity to test and teach Philip. Jesus placed Philip in an impossible situation apart from faith and belief. In this account we see no direct teaching of truth to Philip.

55

Through Discussion

In Mark 4, Jesus teaches to a crowd the parable of the sower. In verse 10, we find that Jesus' followers immediately asked what the parable meant. Jesus had not told them everything they needed to know, opening room for pondering and questions.

> And as soon as He was alone, His followers, along with the twelve, began asking Him about the parables.

After explaining why He taught in parables, Jesus responds to His followers' question by explaining the parable. Jesus frequently taught His disciples through their questions, altering the communication from a lecture style to a discussion with an interested audience who felt free to ask hard questions.

Through Questions

In Matthew16:13-16 Jesus does not tell the disciples what to believe regarding Himself. Instead, He asks them what *they* think.

> Now when Jesus came into the district of Caesarea Philippi, He began asking His disciples, saying "Who do people say that the Son of Man is?" And they said, "Some say John the Baptist; and others, Elijah; but still others, Jeremiah, or one of the prophets." He said to them, "But who do you say that I am?" And Simon Peter answered and said, "Thou art the Christ, the Son of the living God."

In this passage Jesus is drawing the disciples out, first asking who the people said He was, then asking the disciples who they thought He was. This may be the most important question of all time. And it has a pivotal answer. The answer would be vital to the success of Jesus' ministry on earth. Yet in this crucial moment, Jesus asked questions rather than lecturing His disciples. He wanted them to come to this vital truth on their own, not based upon a convincing argument.

Having implemented some of these principles a number of years earlier during our time with Campus Crusade, we had begun to spend more time with our disciples outside of Bible study and the weekly individual discipleship times. We went fishing, had meals together at our home, and got our groups of men and women together for social activities. While these times did not have organized prayer or planned teaching, frequently those things occurred naturally as the interaction and time together developed deeper relationships. Our times together allowed for interaction about real questions and issues related to the truth of Scripture. The fruit of this approach led to four out of six disciples choosing to serve the Lord full time in various ministries around the globe.

Yet now with our church-based college ministry, this approach alone was not yielding the fruit it had before. We took this to mean that there was more to learn from Jesus' ministry with His disciples, so we began a deeper study of Jesus' interaction with the disciples, examining only the passages where Jesus met with *just* His disciples.

We limited our search to these verses because when Jesus spoke to the masses of Israelites, He often sought to show them their inability to reach God under the Law. In fact, in the Sermon on the Mount Jesus took every law to the extreme for this purpose. The level of performance Jesus taught in the Sermon on the Mount was so strict that no one could hope to attain that level of perfection. He wanted to clearly show the people their need for His final sacrifice to stand holy before God. This is evident in this passage as Jesus preaches the Sermon on the Mount.

Matthew 5:27-30

> *You have heard that it was said, "You shall not commit adultery;"*
> *but I say to you that everyone who looks on a woman to lust for*
> *her has committed adultery with her already in his heart. And if*

your right eye makes you stumble, tear it out, and throw it from
you; for it is better for you that one of the parts of your body per-
ish, than for your whole body to be thrown into hell. And if your
right hand makes you stumble, cut it off, and throw it from you;
for it is better for you that one of the parts of your body perish,
than for your whole body to go into hell.

For the men of Israel who needed to live out the Law perfectly, this teaching had to bury them in an impossible expectation. Basically there was no hope for the typical male and they
were likely going to hell. If this were to apply directly to men
in the church today, we would have many blind men without
appendages following Christ.

Several months of study left me somewhat frustrated because
the time with our group of college students became exponentially
more disheartening with every passing week. My growing frustration turned me toward the best outlet, God. I began talking to
Him honestly and frequently throughout the day. After weeks of
calling out to understand what was going on in the lives of these
students, something happened that moved us in a direction that
began to unravel the mystery. One ordinary night Deedee and I
went to bed. I fell straight to sleep without the buzzing of the
never-ending question in my head. At 1:22 a.m., I awoke with
one word frozen in my mind. *Expectation.* It would not leave.
Finally I realized it must tie to my study, but how? Pondering the
word and watching the hours tick by, I was at a complete loss.
Falling back to sleep around 4:00 a.m., I awoke the next morning
with the word *expectation* engraved on my heart. I was troubled
because I could not discern how it fit into my study or the ministry that had Deedee and me on the ropes.

Over the following two weeks the word *expectation* would just
not drift away. Searching for it in the Bible and in Greek, I could
find no parallel word. I still couldn't find a direct tie to our study

or our group. Because this word was so heavy on my mind and heart, I began to hear things differently. Listening to sermons, to our small group lessons, and to my own teaching, there appeared one expectation after another: the way we should think, live, learn, and grow.

This led me to ask individual students in the college ministry, "What do you think is expected of you to be considered a 'good Christian?'" They were stunned by the question and responded to my deep desire to hear from them. They opened up and the list that came together from my seven disciples was long. Then we asked the whole group the question and the list grew even longer.

As Deedee and I reviewed the list we were floored and at the same time weary from just looking at all they perceived was expected of them. It was clear that even we could not live up to all they perceived, and we were their leaders. Since we had tried everything else we knew to do, one Sunday morning we wrote all of the expectations we had received from them on a white board. Seeing the list set the students back in their chairs. When we asked them if the list was accurate from their perspective, they said, "Yes."

We told them that their assignment for the next two weeks was to find verses in the New Testament to support each of these expectations. For the first time in a year and half the students seemed genuinely engaged. We also saw a familiar touch of arrogance in their eyes, as if this would be easy because they had all the answers. As that first Sunday progressed, they could find no verse to support a single one of their first twenty expectations. When we discussed each one and the potential verses to support or refute it, confusion replaced their arrogance. It was as if these expectations were the foundation of their faith, even if they were not living them. All at once that false foundation was removed!

Fast forward twelve years and we have met with fifteen groups of students from multiple churches. These groups are reporting that more than 50 percent of the students feel only somewhat successful in their faith. Many carry significant guilt or have actually grown altogether numb to those feelings.

When students carry a sense of guilt over a long period, it either damages their sense of value as a believer or numbs to their sense of guilt altogether. This numbing presents a real challenge to parents and youth ministers. It's why we hear from both teens and parents that some teens even say go ahead and dish out the consequences because it won't impact them. Many of the college students in our group were in this same position. "Go ahead, try and teach me something new, but it will not affect my life!" This numbness appears to be commonplace in youth ministries across the country.

While wrapping up a recent state youth convention session, a student came up to me after my talk on failure and said he used to feel really guilty about pornography. But, he continued, he was now numb. I asked him if that had led him to look at more and more extreme content. He said, "Yes." As we talked he disclosed that many of his friends were telling him that it was common. They told him that it was a normal male desire that God created. He had spent many days trying to escape pornography without victory. Combined with the input of his friends in youth group, he had become numb to the guilt the Holy Spirit had in place to help him escape something that would impact his life in the future. During our conversation he said to me, "I know it's not right, but I am completely numb and I don't know how to change." The numbness he was encountering deep within was not just affecting his faith and desire to read the Bible, but was impacting him in every area of his life: his relationship with his parents and friends, and even the things he had enjoyed prior to shutting down.

Given all this input, we decided to run some group exercises.

We targeted what students thought was expected of them. We did not anticipate hitting a release valve on a boiler. The pent-up frustration of trying to live up to what they perceived as being expected and the consistent sense of falling short rapidly poured out. In the first group exercise, a room of twenty-five students from six youth groups listed fifty-five expectations in just ten minutes.

Abbreviated list of expectations reported by students[12]

Be Holy	No alcohol	**Do not hang out with sinful people**
Know the whole Bible	No sex	**Always be in a good mood**
Share your faith	No fun	**Always have strong faith**
Defend your faith	No bad language	**Do not back slide**
Read the Bible daily	No secular music	**Be involved/serve**
Pray daily	No dancing	**Always respect your parents**
Pray without ceasing	No parties	**Be the perfect child**

That list is a composite of hundreds of responses from teens and is weighted with the expectations listed that were most frequently reported.

We were astonished that this list was even longer than the

one we had tripped across with our church college ministry years earlier. As we've discussed this list with other students and groups, we've been surprised at how similar the expectations are from church to church and region to region. We consistently hear things that surprise us like… "no hats!" We also find consistent contradictions like "do not hang out with sinful people yet reach your non-Christian friends." As we look at the list and the contradictions, we are forced to ask, "How does that work?" If the list has me asking this question, imagine what postmodern teens are thinking, feeling, and as a result doing—they're leaving the church!

Many of these expectations are not of themselves bad things. But we must question how students already burdened with a hefty list of expectations—real or not—will respond when we teach them more truth with more application points. Will they respond with excitement, joy, and a sense of hope, or with glazed eyes, that may cause us to question whether they are truly believers?

This is the root of my concern toward those who talk about increasing the expectations of our youth. For those who have strong relationships with their leaders, increased expectations may result in apparent change and faith action. But for those without a strong relationship, it might well bury them further. This was the case with the college group Deedee and I led. The students had perceived the many expectations of performance placed on them and had checked out. They came every week but the teaching no longer impacted their lives.

Clearly we need to teach the living Word to our teens, so the issue of expectations creates a genuine dilemma. As we have sought to understand this dilemma, we've also worked to place ourselves back into the mindset of the hormone-crazed, confined world of teens that lends itself to black and white conclusions and a smugness that appears to say "we have this all figured out." Remember those days when everything seemed so clear, when energy was easy to come by—and so was false confidence?

Another trait of the teen years is idealism. Being young and idealistic is not a bad thing. Jesus was the ultimate idealist. He aimed for perfection and actually hit the mark. We need to remember that this youthful idealism has led young people to be the conduit for many major outreaches, awakenings, and mission movements in our country's history. Yet we adults often look down upon those who are young, idealistic, and overconfident. We want to teach them a thing or two. Instead, perhaps we need to embrace them, understand them, work with them, and thereby harness their idealism to move the body of Christ forward.

At the same time, this youthful idealism significantly contributes to the issue of expectations. We've found that teens' idealism causes them to perceive knowledge, and especially the application points we communicate to them, as something that must be accomplished in their lives today, tomorrow, or very soon. Let's look at the math behind this thought process.

A student who attends church, Sunday school, and youth group is likely getting three application points a week. This could be even higher for students attending a Christian school. These numbers do not include application points parents may be trying to accomplish with their student at home. If just one Bible-related application point comes from a parent each week, a student can easily receive four or more a week. If we multiply four by just forty-five weeks, some youth are expected to absorb 180 application points per year!

In a straw poll of mature Christian adults, I asked, "In your best year in how many areas did you see change in your life?" Outside of adult conversions of those with torrid pasts, I heard that adults typically see God change two or three things a year in a good year. Compare this with the sense we often leave with our youth, that they need to be sanctified before they leave our homes. Our desire to keep teens from failure and harm can easily backfire leaving them feeling like everything needs to be right in their lives today. This only results in a list of expectations that they know cannot be reached. What a heavy burden for a young idealistic heart. Their faith walk becomes the exact opposite of what Jesus says in Matthew 11:28-30.

> *Come to Me, all who are weary and heavy-laden, and I will give*
> *you rest. Take My yoke upon you, and learn from Me, for I am*
> *gentle and humble in heart; and you shall find rest for your souls.*
> *For My yoke is easy and My load is light.*

This message would have connected with the Israelites of Jesus' day as they found themselves under the heavy burden and expectation of perfectly living out the Law. This burden of expectations is one of the forces behind what we have come to call the "devil's triangle" that discourages the hearts of our young people.

QUESTIONS AND REFLECTIONS

My wife and I stopped and asked the students in our college ministry why they came. Have you ever stopped and asked yourself the same question? Why do you go to church or small group week in and week out? Write down the reason(s) you attend.

Reflect upon your answers. Are they modern or postmodern in nature? Would your answers keep your teens engaged and coming every week?

What is your predominant approach to your teen? For example: lecturing, telling, discussing, asking questions, or providing experiences?

Reflection

We have seen great fruit in the lives of our teens by asking them questions and involving them in the process of structuring the day. Asking questions like, what do you think is reasonable regarding the amount of time spent on the Internet? Or, when you leave home, how often do you think you will need to clean your apartment to keep it presentable in case a guy or girl drops by? Questions involve them and give them a voice in the decisions that are made. This helps them feel more in control of their destiny and trains them to think and make good decisions for the day when they will be on their own.

What does your student perceive as expected of them in order to consider themselves successful in their faith?

List out the expectations you think your teen and/or group is carrying?

Do you believe the list of expectations your young person is carrying is achievable?

What do you believe is the foundation of your teen's faith: knowledge, expectation, performance, or an inner desire to follow the Lord?

CHAPTER FIVE

THE DEVIL'S TRIANGLE

Many of us are familiar with the lore of the Devil's Triangle, also known as the Bermuda Triangle. It's an imaginary area off the southeast coast of the United States, noted for a high incidence of unexplained disappearances of ships and aircraft. In 1945, Flight 19, consisting of a squadron of five TBM Avenger Torpedo Bombers, while in radio contact with the tour became confused, fell silent, and disappeared. Today, it seems that we are losing entire squadrons of young people who were in contact with us, seemed to be doing well, and then all of a sudden silently disappeared.

Some want to question the faith or salvation of those who leave the church, believing that if they were true believers they would not have grown so distant and cared so little about the truth we have taught them. Clearly there are unbelievers in our youth groups, but to conclude that a majority of the loss is a result of kids who grew up in the church and did not become true believers points us toward only one set of conclusions and solutions.

Through our time with young people, we believe that many that leave are indeed believers who made "child-like" faith decisions in Sunday school, at VBS, or at camp. Their young hearts were open to the Lord and they asked questions about God. But somewhere between ages nine and thirteen, their hearts start to vanish into our own version of the Devil's Triangle, much like the airplanes did in the Bermuda Triangle.

While the disappearance of the heart may appear sudden to a parent or youth worker, the opposite is actually true. Just think about the last time you attempted to bury something, especially if that object was not flat but had a number of high spots. It took shovelful after shovelful before finally that last load completely covered the item and it vanished from sight.

Our kids' hearts are not flat. Indeed, they're unlike any inanimate object. Our kids' hearts are actually fighting for life and light. Over time many factors beyond their control toss load after load upon their hearts until at last the fight is over; their hearts are completely obscured. The good news is that the heart infused with the Lord does not die even when buried six feet underground. That heart is there waiting and hoping, and can be unearthed.

As we have analyzed the conversations and videotaped interviews with teens, we have found a spiritual version of the Devil's Triangle at work. We've come to call this the Triangle of Discouragement.

The bedrock for the triangle is identified by George Gallup Jr., the famous researcher who has helped many corporations successfully connect their products and services with our young people. Gallup is quoted as saying:

Sadly, parents and adults in general tend to view young people in a negative light, overlooking their truly positive characteristics. Much of this negativism stems from a lack of awareness and knowledge about the lives and aspirations of youth. [13]

In this quote we discover truth even within the body of Christ. Many parents joke and talk about the challenge of their kids heading for the teenage years. These years are seen as hard, risky, and something not joyfully anticipated. Further, teens' thoughts, ideas, and desires are often not given much credence within the leadership structure of their local church because they are young, idealistic, and inexperienced. This is sadly ironic when one looks at our nation's history and finds that often major mission movements and awakenings come from our young people.

This general negative perception of young people in our country and our churches is not missed by our youth. It serves as the basis for the three components of the Triangle of Discouragement, which can make the hearts of our youth vanish before our eyes.

Many influences act on the lives of our young people today. Three of these together consume the majority of a young person's productive time: parents, school, and church/church related activities. Each desires to develop young people into mature, responsible adults. Within the realm of each is an additional influence, the community of students and friends who are part of the organization. They emphasize the importance of the culture that exists among the students in these environments. As we've discussed these influences with teens, we've discovered a disconnect between the mission of these three influences and the students' perception and interaction with them.

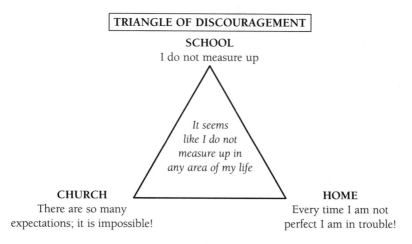

TRIANGLE OF DISCOURAGEMENT

SCHOOL
I do not measure up

It seems like I do not measure up in any area of my life

CHURCH
There are so many
expectations; it is impossible!

HOME
Every time I am not
perfect I am in trouble!

One of the significant influences in the lives of teens is school. We've found that a minority of students in school, whether public, private, or Christian feel believed in, trusted, or empowered to believe that they will accomplish great things. Often students get a sense from these environments that they do not measure up; they find themselves not feeling smart enough, athletic enough, pretty enough, or funny enough. Only a few are blessed to be so gifted in one way or another that they receive the kudos that help them believe they can accomplish great things in the future, in the world, or for the Lord.

Many students struggle to meet expectations across a broad range of topics, some outside their interests. It is often difficult for some to accept the way they were created by God. These factors, combined with activities like P.E. and negative social interactions, cause them to question their value. For some this leads to a sense of hopelessness related to their abilities and the future. The first leg of the Triangle of Discouragement has been established.

Second, our students are involved at church or in a youth ministry where they report they are taught basically how to avoid all sin, be pure, study the Bible, pray daily, and be holy. They know these are true and often have tried to make them a reality in their lives, only to fall short over and over again. As they mature, they discover that they are unable to live the sinless life they have been encouraged to lead. They're hit by temptation and often failure in one or more areas. While they make earnest efforts to meet the expectations, they also begin to transfer the origin of these expectations from us to God. As they continue falling short, they perceive that they cannot possibly please God. This belief combined with the general mistrust of teens and the sense that they are to be present but not heard creates the second leg of the Triangle of Discouragement.

Finally, students head home to their parents looking for

someone who will believe in them, trust them, and empower them to tackle the future on their own. As parents, we often miss this opportunity due to our teens' change in approach to us and because of our own busyness. Many parents have recounted stories about their teens saying, "you don't trust me." Our students are seeking to be empowered, believed in, and trusted like Jesus exhibited with His young disciples.

Our young people pick up on our expectations quickly. At home they often are met with another set of expectations tied to their future: their music or sports and their life as a Christian. This is the area where we often find the greatest frustration among teens. The failure to meet expectations at home weighs heavily upon their hearts. In every session held with students related to expectations, a good percentage indicated the need to be "the perfect child." Some rebel; others become very good at acting the part. It seems that every time they don't look and sound Christian, another lecture is on the way; every time they make a mistake or forget to be responsible some privilege or responsibility is removed. As a result, they excel at hiding their failures. This directly leads into the intentionally deceptive dual life that appears to plague our ministries. This third leg completes the Triangle of Discouragement.

As students perceive society's general negative view of young people, and sense that view is confirmed at school, church, and unintentionally at home, they grow numb and tune adults out because they cannot withstand the sense of falling short at every turn. Each message received communicates, "you do not measure up, are not believed in, or are not trusted." This can become another load of dirt thrown on a heart already struggling to develop its identity. The process of burying a heart can begin at an early age with young impressionable hearts closing to parents as early as age nine. This was the case with our first daughter.

She was an over-achiever, reading by age four. She completed the novel Charlotte's Web *in just a week in kindergarten. Her incredible intellect was also her greatest weakness. By age two and a half, she could already debate and frequently win battles with her mother. We like many others had been through* Growing Kids God's Way *and were lovingly disciplining her to help her grow up in the way of the Lord. This worked when she was young and it altered her behavior, so we thought we were doing well. The maxim 'spare the rod, spoil the child' is true, but it does not indicate where the age of childhood ends and how parents should proceed from that point forward.*

As our daughter grew older we noticed that she was having a harder and harder time admitting she was wrong. By age nine, she would blame the wind, the dog, her sister, or anything to avoid being wrong. This weighed heavily on my heart. Through some very difficult times I had rediscovered how important it was to be able to look inward into my own heart and soul to see real spiritual growth occur. Watching my daughter avoid admitting fault at any cost broke my heart because she could no longer look inward and self-evaluate in an open and honest way.

The place where the Holy Spirit resides in her was shut down and unwilling to open to see its role in the issues that were becoming more and more evident in her life. Her precious little heart that once prompted her to remind us to pray at meals and to bring her children's Bible to us to read was gone. It took us a while to realize that the issue was not hers but ours; we had unintentionally shut her precious little heart down with our approach to her mistakes and shortcomings as she grew older! Having altered our approach for several years now, we have seen her heart reemerge and can observe the fruit of a heart that is able to look at her own faults within.

The Triangle of Discouragement is a silent killer lurking behind what we see and often beyond what our pre-teens and teens understand. Their young identities and hearts are seeking validation. Often, the only thing giving them a sense of being believed in, trusted, and valued for who they are, in spite of their faults, is their friends who are leading a dual life or are outside the church.

This killer is frequently driven by the way we approach students with the truth, and is in sharp contrast with how Jesus taught truth. In Mark 7:5-8 we read of Jesus responding to the Pharisees regarding His not following the tradition of the elders. Jesus' response targets the heart and challenges their teaching.

And the Pharisees and the scribes asked Him, "Why do Your disciples not walk according to the tradition of the elders, but eat their bread with impure hands?" And He said to them, "Rightly did Isaiah prophesy of you hypocrites, as it is written, 'This people honors me with their lips, but their heart is far away from me; but in vain do they worship Me, teaching as doctrines the precepts of men.' Neglecting the commandment of God, you hold to the tradition of men."

Some expectations we place upon our young people are pointing toward holy living, but others being taught as doctrine may not have a true biblical basis at all; they're commandments of men.

Jesus approached teaching His disciples very differently than He did the masses. With the masses, He took the Law to an extreme using the heavy expectations of following the Law perfectly to show that it was impossible and that they would need His once-for-all sacrifice.

In the case of the disciples, we find that He removed the external expectation of the Law, instead frequently seeking an internal desire from the disciples to follow and to grow.

Is this the way that we approach our youth with the amazing truth of God? Do they see the loving hand of God as a distant ruler with many requirements? Could these expectations be having the same impact upon the hearts of our youth as the Law had upon the Israelites and their spiritual leaders, the Pharisees? Jesus called them whitewashed tombs (Matt. 23:27) because they looked good on the outside but were living a very different life when not in the spotlight. This is much like the deceptive dual life we are seeing so prominently among our youth.

Jesus knew that truly "Great Expectations" flow from within, based upon the internal desire of an individual to care, love, and serve. Genuine love is not based upon a marriage license or a law, but comes from a heart in tune with its Maker.

CHAPTER SIX

GREAT EXPECTATIONS

A t the time I had no idea the importance of the lesson God revealed in the fall of 1990. For nearly a year and a half God had kept Mike on my heart. It began my first semester on campus as a college minister when Mike filled out a spiritual interest card. It was my first year of direct, one-on-one discipleship based ministry and Mike presented a unique challenge. He was an only child from an isolated town. His first year on campus was overwhelming. Socially, he was a fish out of water. Mike was surrounded by 20,000 students, most of whom came from much larger schools and cities. He found himself having a hard time relating and was lonely in spite of being in a fraternity.

Working with Mike was an exercise in obedience, not one of love or joy. He was a member of a fraternity with an odd reputation, so I had real concern that entering this house on a regular basis would prevent my ministry from flourishing in more popular frat houses. Yet God kept sending me to meet with Mike week after week. I battled with this internally because it was so hard to relate to him. He did not look like a future ministry leader in any way, shape, or form. Mike was a sporadic attendee at our ministry's weekly meeting and of my discipleship group.

As the first semester with Mike progressed there was no breakthrough. Having been solely focused on his spiritual life, I failed to recognize the struggles going on in the rest of his life. By the end of that first semester Mike had failed many of his classes and was unable to return for the second semester.

I was surprised when Mike called me the following fall. He was back and wanted to continue to meet with me one-on-one. I'm sure he was just lonely. My struggle with investing in Mike grew as that semester progressed. He continued to be inconsistently involved, his schoolwork consumed him, and I saw no apparent desire for God. Toward the end of that semester we were sitting in his room at the frat house as Mike finished a project on his Apple Macintosh, the one that looked like a shoe box set on its end with a little screen. If there was one thing in the world Mike felt at home with and was devoted to, it was his Mac.

To this day, apart from the leading of God's Spirit, I cannot explain what came out of my mouth. It was one of the greatest lessons God ever taught me in ministry. As I sat watching him type away, I said, "Mike, you know you could use that computer for God." This got his attention more than anything I had ever taught him from Scripture. He stopped, turned, and asked, "What?"

I repeated, "You could use your computer for God."

"How?" he wanted to know. I explained that Campus Crusade was great at working with students like myself but not with people like Mike. As a result, every year staff who wanted to work on campus were diverted to serve at headquarters doing various jobs including computer work.

Mike restated it. "You mean I could go on staff with Campus Crusade and work on computers?" When I answered yes it was if a switch flipped. I had no idea how significant that switch had been. That afternoon Mike found a purpose that the Spirit must have been impressing on him for some time.

Following that meeting Mike attended every discipleship group study and most weekly meetings. That involvement led him to go on retreats where he heard about a short-term mission trip to Japan. This one-semester trip required fund raising and other things that stretched his faith, but he felt God's call to go. Mike discovered that his personality and thought process fit perfectly in Japan. After graduation, Mike went to seminary and became a senior pastor who returned to Japan to lead a church in his denomination!

This was a powerful lesson that took several years to unfold. The first year of my time with Mike focused on teaching Scripture and getting him involved in the ministry. Mike and I met, but there was not much fruit. Mike, like many young people, had a great deal of knowledge from growing up in the church, but had seen little purpose or use for who he was in the body of Christ or in serving God. He had no purpose and thus felt he had no great value. While he gained more knowledge, he virtually did not grow until his purpose was unearthed.

Mike had grown up in a Christian home and had been in Sunday school every week. He believed in the Lord, but where was the evidence of that in his life? The analogy that helps me understand this phenomenon is found at every fast food restaurant in America; a straw. If you take a straw you can blow an incredible amount of air or content through it. Yet when you place your thumb against one end and blow into the straw, only so much air enters before the back pressure becomes so great no more air can be blown in and it begins to leak out around your lips.

In many ways this was Mike. He'd had content crammed into him for years, but there was no outlet. The back pressure became so great that there was little affect in his life from any additional teaching. In Scripture we see that believers are to be vessels. 2 Timothy 2:21 says:

> *Therefore, if a man cleanses himself from these things, he will be a vessel for honor, sanctified, useful to the Master, prepared for every good work.*

A blood vessel is much like a straw. If its flow is obstructed, blood does not get to the tissue beyond the obstruction. Cells die. Much like a straw, we as believers need to have an outlet for all we are learning. With young people in the church this is rarely the case, unless they are one of the few who can play an instrument or sing. Once Mike had a potential purpose and outlet for his faith, his internal desire came alive. For the first time since his early days as a believer he began to desire internally to learn and grow.

Expectation is a loaded word as we saw in chapter four. Students are frequently carrying so many expectations placed upon them by others that they believe there is no way they can live out their faith. This causes many to give up and leave the church.

Jesus was the Master of great expectations in the lives of His disciples. To understand this we must first understand the nature and meaning of the word *expectation*, which unlocks truly great expectations.

Expectation

1. A confident belief or strong hope that a particular event will happen
2. A mental image of something expected, often compared to its reality (often used in the plural)
3. A standard of conduct or performance expected by or of somebody (often used in the plural)[14]

Examining the definitions of expectation, several analogies shed practical light on these textbook definitions.

1. The first definition might best be understood through the eyes of a child at Christmas time. The child believes the event will happen and cannot wait for the day to come. The internal desire of the child for the day is so strong that the clock seems to slow down and the calendar barely moves. We can all remember those exciting days in our lives or in the lives of our children.
2. A woman expecting a child illuminates the second definition. She has seen other babies and has an expectant look in her eyes, in spite of the inevitable pain the birth will bring. Her

deep internal desire for the day comes as result of having seen other babies and a deep maternal desire to have her baby in her arms.

3. A rule or law may best describe the third definition of the word *expectation*. Rules and laws are created to control the conduct or performance of others. Failure to live up to the rule or law frequently results in a consequence. This is consistent with the third definition. Jesus entered a culture ruled by the Old Testament Law that needed to be performed or required a sacrifice.

Speaking to a group of men recently, I asked them to discuss the word *expectation* and what it meant. The vast majority of their reflections were consistent with the third definition: a standard of conduct or performance expected by or of somebody. We have found that this is also true of youth across our country. Youth see the word *expectation* as needing to perform for or alter their conduct for other people ... or else.

The culture where Jesus began His ministry was ruled by the third definition of expectation. The Roman Empire was the most affluent of its day, so much so that it passed laws increasing taxes on dual income families to attempt to keep people at home with their kids. They recognized the decay taking place from within. The expectations of the culture placed an ever-increasing pressure on people to succeed in a worldly context, much like our culture today.

The Israelites also had a culture of expectations in the form of a code of conduct to be followed or a sacrifice to be made in accordance with the Law. This approach to faith was governed by an external motivation to do what was right. Under this system, Israel went in and out of cycles of apostasy. Each time, God would bring other nations to subjugate Israel. Then He would send a deliverer who brought the nation back in line with His plan.

Ultimately the nation of Israel found itself a culture of white-washed tombs, a people not graced with a prophet from God for 400 years because of their distance from Him. The silence of the prophets did not end until John the Baptist appeared, calling out the way for the Lord.

Jesus entered the culture as the second prophet in 400 years. The expectations of what Jesus would do were high. Those Jews, like previous generations, were hoping He would lead them out from under Roman control, returning them to strong independence. Jesus could have easily called the people back to living under the strict rule of the Law. Yet we find that He approached his disciples differently, focusing not on performance of the Law but upon truly Great Expectations that rise from within.

This is seen in the interactions Jesus had with the Pharisees where they consistently accused Him and His disciples of breaking the Law. To accomplish His mission in the lives of His disciples, Jesus knew He needed a different approach. He did not follow the rules-based teaching model of the synagogue which was based upon teaching and debating the Law in the classroom environment of the Temple. Instead Jesus' teaching often came as a result of an encounter with real people that broke the rules of the Pharisees!

The focus of Jesus' ministry with His disciples was completely incomprehensible to the leadership of the day. Jesus led not by expectations of performance, but rather by seeking to develop the internal desire of His disciples to follow and live out their faith!

In Luke 11:1 we get a glimpse of Jesus' target in the lives of His disciples. It was not the performance of the activities of the faith, but the internal desire to involve the practices in their daily lives, Luke records:

And it came about that while He was praying in a certain place, after He had finished, one of His disciples said to Him, "Lord, teach us to pray just as John also taught his disciples."

The disciples came to Jesus and asked to be taught to pray. Remember this happened *before* Jesus taught them how to pray. Imagine for a second walking with the Lord, your teacher, and thinking, "Why has He not taught us how to pray?" Imagine the discussion between the disciples, "Should we go ask Him to teach us how to pray? He is our rabbi, our teacher. Is it our place to ask? Are we suggesting that He is not doing His job?" It must have taken some time and courage to approach Jesus and ask Him to teach them how to pray.

Our teens helped me begin to reexamine this passage with a different mindset when they asked questions like, "Why did they have to ask Jesus to teach them to pray?" The only logical conclusion I could reach is that Jesus had removed the five daily prayers required in the synagogues for His young disciples. Given that they had been raised in the temple, His disciples would have been schooled in these required prayers. These prayers were spaced throughout the day and required temple goers to stop, face the temple and pray either the Shema or the Prayer of the Eighteen Benedictions twice and three times a day, respectively. Failure to do so was a sin and would be noticed by others as they would come to a halt throughout the day at the appointed times for prayer.

If they had still been praying these prayers, would they have had either the desire or the courage to go ask to be taught to pray? Probably not. As a result, it seems likely that Jesus, upon assembling the disciples, might have said something like, "What do you think of the Shema and Prayer of the Eighteen Benedictions?" Perhaps receiving a lukewarm response to this ritual He may have said, "Well, since they do not seem to be working for you and do not mean much to you, just stop doing them. You are with the Son of Man now so you do not need to turn to the Temple." This of course is all speculation and not directly contained in the Bible, but it helps make sense as we seek to understand why the disciples would have to ask Jesus to teach them to pray. When

Jesus told them they could stop, imagine their response; it probably was two-fold. "Thank you. We have not meant those prayers in years; we were just going through the motions." Second, they may have asked, "What will everyone think of us when the city stops and prays, and we are among only a few who do not turn toward the temple and pray?"

Today I find that we teach our students to pray and then instruct them about having a daily prayer time to draw close to the Lord and grow in their faith. In Scripture we see that the disciples grew without praying daily. Without the ritual to perform, a need built deep within the soul of man went to work. It was "the God-shaped vacuum in the heart of every man" that Pascal describes. When they were no longer filling that need with what had become a meaningless performance, the true power of God was able to work deep within. This inner working of God meshed with the disciples' observing John's disciples praying very differently, with sincerity and joy. They also witnessed that Jesus frequently slipped away to pray. Together these factors resulted in their growing desire to pray. Spiritual growth occurred in them without praying or being taught a lesson about the need to pray! In fact their desire was so great they eventually went to their rabbi, Jesus, and said, "Teach us how to pray as John's disciples pray." Wouldn't it warm our hearts if our youth came to us and asked the same question? Jesus' ministry targeted internal desire consistent with the first two definitions of expectation.

Expectation

1. A confident belief or strong hope that a particular event will happen i.e., a child at Christmas
2. A mental image of something expected, often compared to its reality (often used in the plural) i.e., an expectant mother

It is these definitions that form the basis of the truly Great

Expectations Jesus targeted. They led to the disciples' own internal desire to pray, serve, love, and ultimately sacrifice their lives. Expectations placed upon someone by another may be met because the person wants to please their leader, but will they endure once the leader is gone? Jesus shunned the performance expectations the Pharisees had and instead targeted the internal desire of His disciples so that upon His departure they would continue in their faith and ministry and therefore change the world.

We can confirm this approach, seeking internal desire rather than external performance, from the very beginning of Jesus' ministry when He called His disciples. Jesus' call was not based upon the knowledge and performance of the disciples, but on their internal desire to follow Him. Jesus knew that the approach found in the synagogue had failed. Instead He granted and the disciples found in His presence great freedom from the many expectations that existed in their religious system. Jesus understood well that such freedom would allow growth in God's timing according to what He targeted in the lives of His followers.

Seeking internal desire represents the greatest challenge to the way we currently approach young people in the faith. They find themselves under a pile of expectations consistent with the third definition of expectation: an expectation placed upon a person by someone else. As a result, they never find freedom in Christ. They *become enslaved* by trying to live out all they know in their own power. In this vein they are not allowed to develop an internal desire to follow but are often required to follow or else!

Balancing our need to teach truth and develop the internal desire of our young people is a challenge. Our young people indicate that their knowledge often creates performance expectations and as a result, they do not want to open their Bibles and see more ways they do not measure up. The gap between what they know and how they live creates a disconnect and sense of falling short that forms the "Knowledge Dilemma."

QUESTIONS AND REFLECTIONS

George Gallup said,

Sadly, parents and adults in general tend to view young people in a negative light, overlooking their truly positive characteristics. Much of this negativism stems from a lack of awareness and knowledge about the lives and aspirations of youth.

Do you truly view young people positively or negatively? Why?

How does that view impact your relationship with your teen and his or her friends?

The definition of expectation leans more toward the internal desire of a person for something than a standard of required conduct. Did the definition of expectation change your perspective regarding how young people are approached? If so, how?

Are the young people in your life performing to meet your expectations or do they have an internal desire to follow the faith and life practices desired beyond your front door?

How can you help your young people become an open straw through which the knowledge or outcomes we desire in their lives can be used in a manner that will engage them?

How can you begin to balance the need to teach truth with developing the internal desire of your young person to do what is good, right, and true in their life?

CHAPTER SEVEN

THE KNOWLEDGE DILEMMA

———⟨⟨⟨⟨⟨ ⟩⟩⟩⟩⟩———

*J*ohn *came to faith late in life when he was twenty-eight years old. His conversion was fairly radical and his hunger for the Word was ferocious. He participated in two Bible studies a week, attended church, and was in an accountability group. The pace of his learning was staggering. For a season many of John's pre-Christ issues were gone as if by magic, wrapped up in the excitement and busyness of his new life. We were excited to have a small role in his coming to the Lord, but as time progressed Deedee and I became concerned. We had witnessed this course with new converts several times before. The excitement of salvation and forgiveness is wonderful. Many late converts go on a sort of knowledge binge and expectations pile up quickly. We were concerned that John was running headlong down the trail toward a brick wall of personal discouragement.*

We were fortunate to spend some extended time with him around the one-year anniversary of his becoming a believer. His rapid knowledge growth was evident, but with it came an attitude that worried us. He was gaining an air of confidence and arrogance related to the Scripture and God. As we talked with him, he wanted to debate many points of fact. We warned him that young believers often learn so quickly that they experience a crash. He did not heed our warning.

About six months later John stopped attending his two Bible studies. He was disillusioned with the faith ostensibly because of what he saw going on around him. He had grown rigid in his belief of what was right and wrong. In his excitement and fervor for the Lord he had been able to temporarily overcome sins that had previously entangled him. Now some of them were returning. It greatly bothered him that with all he knew and his natural, strong self-controlled personality, he could not defeat them. He battled them in a silent personal war of attrition and was losing. The strong confidence of his faith in what was true, right, and wrong and his Christian image made it necessary for him to hide his sin. His knowledge had kept growing, yet the pace of his spiritual growth had not kept up. A disconnect within drove him back into the darkness.

One evening, alone in his apartment, John concluded that his faith was not working. He felt guilty and alone and missed the openness of his non-Christian friends. He wondered why he should keep pretending. It was not long before he found himself back in his former world, not to bring glory to God but to escape into the comfort of his life before Christ. He was soon attending church numb to the teaching and living a very different life with his co-workers Monday morning through Saturday night. His guilt lingered quietly in the background, drowned out by the sense of acceptance the world had to offer. Now nine years later he still battles the demons that existed before He accepted Christ. He is alone, held powerless in his faith by the lack of life change that he had believed occurred in the fervor of his first year in Christ.

This is the crux of the knowledge dilemma. Knowledge growth does not always equate with spiritual growth. Clearly knowledge is important and even vital in our ability to grow as believers. But as we interact with teens and parents, far too often we find teens have a great deal of knowledge, yet their lives are far from aligning with it. The difference leaves them feeling like something is wrong with them, their faith, or both. Many teens we interviewed have tried in vain to have regular quiet times or prayer times, or to overcome some sin that reappears from deep within time and time again. They fall short in spite of their knowledge, effort, and many years of walking with the Lord.

Today knowledge and expectation are inseparably tied to our culture. Our culture places many performance expectations upon us in unseen ways. They factor in what we do, how we look, our activities, and whether or not we attain success. The western mindset that has dominated much of the past century has told us that knowledge and information are power. Because it is deeply engrained within us, we fall prey to the "know it, do it" syndrome in spite of the simple fact that we can acquire knowledge much more quickly than deep life change can occur within us. Our nation's rugged, independent mindset of pulling ourselves up by our own bootstraps can seep into our faith. Then, when this approach does not work with our faith, some of us are left with unnerving questions and often hidden failure.

This was the case with John and with many of our young people today. In many instances we have taught our youth about grace, but they have not experienced it in the spheres within which they live.

Today the focus on knowledge-related solutions to the loss of youth from the church and the general malaise of much of the body of Christ is clear. Apologetics, worldview, and deeper doctrinal training are frequently touted as the answer. Yet when I speak with adults I often ask for a show of hands of how many individuals know more than they are currently applying? The response is always unanimous; 100 percent raise their hands. Then I ask, "If I teach you more knowledge right now, is that going to change you?" With almost stunned faces they shake their heads, no.

Given our modern mindset that values knowledge, reason, and higher education, it's easy to see how we can fall prey to the knowledge dilemma, believing that the dissemination of knowledge in and of itself will bring about life change. Even if we do not believe that, when we examine our ministries, one might conclude that this is our belief given the way our ministries function.

This leads to another question. Exactly how much knowledge is enough?

In one of my early meetings with Bill Tell, Senior Vice President and Chief of Staff of The Navigators, we discussed building a coalition of ministries to address the loss of youth. Rather quickly, we found ourselves in a discussion about knowledge. As I shared some of my observations, his concern increased and he responded very graciously that he felt knowledge was vitally important. I assured him that I agreed with him, but that it seemed like we, as moderns, were out of balance between our love of knowledge and other aspects of spiritual growth.

We shared more thoughts. Then, I asked this burning question for the very first time, "How much knowledge is enough?" I will never forget how Bill sat back, got an almost amused look on his face, stopped to think and said, "That is a great question!" As the conversation continued we mused about it together. Bill shared he'd had numerous days when he felt that he was more effective for the Lord in the early days of his ministry with the Navigators when he knew just a fraction of what he knows today. Thus began a dialogue that has continued for several years related to knowledge and spiritual growth.

How knowledge affected Paul

One of the chief verses speaking about knowledge is 2 Timothy 2:15. Paul tells Timothy:

> *Be diligent to present yourself approved to God as a workman*
> *who does not need to be ashamed, handling accurately the word*
> *of truth.*

What did Paul mean? Could it have meant to Paul and Timothy what it has come to mean to us today: systematic theology, apologetics, worldview, or a seminary degree?

To understand this fully we must first attempt to understand the author. Paul, although a scholar of the Old Testament when he wrote this to Timothy, appears to be keenly aware of both the upside and downside of knowledge. Although Paul was a recognized scholar in the Old Testament, his heart had strayed far from God to the point where he too was a Pharisee who would have been called a whitewashed tomb by Jesus.

Paul excelled in his study of Scripture and in his faith, saying he had outdone his contemporaries in Philippians 3:4-6.

If anyone else has a mind to put confidence in the flesh, I far more: circumcised the eighth day, of the nation of Israel, of the tribe of Benjamin, a Hebrew of Hebrews; as to the Law, a Pharisee; as to zeal, a persecutor of the church; as to the righteousness which is in the Law, found blameless.

In spite of all his knowledge and faith, Paul harbored enough hate in his heart to murder. His encounter with Jesus on the Damascus road, his subsequent healing from blindness, and his extended period out of circulation taught him a great deal that he had apparently missed in his previous study of Scripture.

Up to the time of his first missionary journey it would make sense that Paul was recovering from his previous misdirection. Wrestling with his knowledge of the Old Testament, guilt, shame, and the reality of grace appear to have helped him reassess what was truly important. Clearly Paul still saw knowledge as important, but he saw it differently after his life-changing encounter with Jesus.

We get a glimpse of how his view of knowledge changed when Paul wrote 1 Corinthians 13:1-2.

*If I speak with the tongues of men and of angels, but do not have love, I have become a noisy gong or a clanging cymbal. If I have the gift of prophecy, and know all the mysteries and **all knowledge**;*

*and if I have **all faith**, so as to remove mountains, but do not have love, I am nothing (emphasis added).*

Paul is pointing to the futility of wisdom, knowledge and even faith if it's not rooted in love. Today love seems to be a lost art in our country and our church. Laying down one's own life for a friend goes a lot further than we are frequently comfortable with, yet this was the definition of love Jesus gave to the disciples in His final teaching time with them. He declared in John 15:12-13:

This is my commandment, that you love one another, just as I have loved you. Greater love has no one than this, that one lay down his life for his friends.

Even in the Old Testament, the word *love* appears four times more often than the combination of the words *truth* and *knowledge*. And though Paul had great knowledge of the Scriptures, the word *love*, and its pivotal role in our relationship with God, he found himself capable of killing to protect what he believed was scriptural truth. We observe a similar disconnect between the knowledge of Scripture and the actions of men with Christians in the period of the Crusades as well. We must conclude that knowledge of the truth does not change the heart of man. Neither do laws. We can pass a law that says do not murder. But does the law change the heart of a man and prevent hate from building up in his heart to the point of killing? Clearly the answer is no.

Returning to Paul's pivotal teaching regarding love in 1 Cor. 13, we see a concluding emphasis in verses 8-12:

*Love never fails; but if there are gifts of prophecy, they will be done away; if there are tongues, they will cease; **if there is knowledge, it will be done away. For we know in part** and we prophesy in part; but when the perfect comes, the partial will be done away. When I was a child, I used to speak as a child, think as a child,*

reason as a child; when I became a man, I did away with childish
things. For now we see in a mirror dimly, but then face to face;
now I know in part, *but then I will know fully just as I also have*
been fully known (emphasis added).

Knowledge in part

Paul, a scholar of the Old Testament, admitted that the knowledge he had, he had in part. This was a humbling admission for a Pharisee and one of the brightest scriptural minds of the day. This is a confession I am confident he would not have made prior to meeting Jesus on the Damascus road. He went on to say in this passage that knowledge will pass away, but faith, hope, and love will remain!

Paul had discovered that he was never going to fully grasp the height nor depth of the love of God (Rom. 8:38-39) and all the mysteries around how He works in the world. In place of his very apparent effort to be considered one of the top scholars of his faith as a Pharisee, he altered his course, becoming one who would take beating after beating in city after city to become all things to all men that he might win a few. It is this self-sacrifice predicated upon the love of his fellow countrymen that we admire even more than his doctrinal treatise of Romans. This helps us understand that while Paul valued knowledge, he saw it as only part of the equation. When we talk about being an approved workman of the word, do we see it in the same light as Paul?

Studying Romans for a year and a half, verse by verse, led me to the same conclusion. After battling with the weightiness of the "potter and the clay" and chapter 7, verses 15 and 24, "Oh what a wretched man I am for I do what I do not want to do," one arrives at Romans 13:8. Paul sums it all up:

Owe nothing to anyone except to love one another; for he who
loves his neighbor has fulfilled the law.

If we stop and consider this simple verse, it is profound. If we love our neighbors, will we steal from them? If we love our wives, will we have an affair? If we love our neighbors, will we covet what is theirs? Paul, this highly educated Pharisee, sums up the Christian faith so simply. It must have been difficult for his former friends and fellow Pharisees to understand or comprehend.

Advice for a young preacher

This background gives us an understanding of Paul and his journey leading up to his writing letters to his young friend, Timothy. In the second letter, chapter 2, verse 15, we read:

> *Be diligent to present yourself approved to God as a workman*
> *who does not need to be ashamed, accurately handling the word of*
> *truth.*

When Paul urged Timothy to accurately handle the word of truth, what was he saying? It is important to remember that Timothy was both young and a head pastor who needed to instruct older men. Few today find themselves in Timothy's position. When we seek to understand the meaning of this passage we must also place it in the time of its writing.

Paul wrote to Timothy as his spiritual son. The New Testament did not exist, nor did systematic theology, worldview, or apologetics. What existed were some circulating letters, oral stories of Jesus, and the Old Testament scrolls in the synagogue. It is difficult to conclude that Paul was telling Timothy to get a seminary degree or develop an approach to systematic theology. What Timothy had to work with was a mere fraction of what we possess.

Today we have online sermons, radio programs, tens of thousands of books, commentaries, and study tools, not to mention the New Testament. Again, none of this existed when Paul wrote to Timothy, "Be an approved workman of the Word." Few had access to the Old Testament scrolls; they were not mass-produced and available to someone like Timothy.

Fewer still had access to the letters of the apostles. We have the privilege of personally owning a Bible, if not multiple different Bible translations including an electronic version on our cell phones. This is not the case for much of the church in the world today. Many are not fortunate enough to have their own Bible. Yet in these places, we often find incredibly loving and faithful people operating with a simple childlike faith that convicts us. They listen on Sunday and live for the Lord throughout the week. Many who go overseas on short-term missions and visit these churches are amazed by the joy and faith of these people.

Why is it with all our knowledge that we do not look like we have the faith, fervor, and commitment of those overseas who have far less knowledge than we do? We must ask, "Could this passage have meant to Timothy what it has come to mean for us as modern leaders today: systematic theology, worldview, and apologetics?" These are all tools designed for modern thinkers that were needed to reach people of the age in which they lived. They are strategic for mature postmodern teens that have crossed the faith gap of experience and truth because they have witnessed God's work in their lives and are ready to take the intellectual side of their understanding of the faith deeper.

It is likely that those of us who have grown up in the church or have been believers for three or four years, listening to sermons and participating in small groups, probably have as much or more knowledge than Timothy who was already a head pastor. After teaching the Scripture for twenty years, I clearly see that my teaching does not change people. Is knowledge important? Yes! "How will they believe in Him whom they have not heard?" (Rom.10:14). However, Jesus did far more than just teach the truth to shape His disciples into men who would change the world.

Approaching our postmodern youth

Our modern predisposition for truth and knowledge leads us to reach our young people through lecturing in a classroom setting. This closely resembles the synagogue's approach to teaching young people in Jesus' time. Jesus came into that culture with a different approach and had thousands following Him around the countryside. He did not use the ordained system of the day and as a result Jesus was not popular with the church leadership.

For us as modern leaders to say that the way we approach the faith is the only right way and to teach our youth to follow only our model is to overlook the reality of our current culture. Our country has walked away from God on our watch and under our approach to the faith.

As I have wrestled with this reality, my seminary training and the trials God has brought my way have helped me look differently at the splendor of Jesus' ministry. Like Paul, I have begun to see Jesus' love and His shepherding of the disciples as paramount in developing young people who will stick to the faith and lead us into a ministry model that can touch the lives of people today. Jesus' approach was not purely built on lecture, Bible study, knowledge, rules, and consequences.

Jesus' teaching and teaching style were radically different than that found in the synagogue and it drew criticism from many, yet it was founded 100 percent upon the truth. Jesus frequently used questions, often without providing answers, to cause people to think. Reviewing Scripture, there appears to be no passage where Jesus developed detailed arguments for holding to the Old Testament as truth or for the existence of God. These things were not a core need of a pre-modern thinker as they have been for modern thinkers. Today the map is shifting again. We find that young people are highly spiritual but disconnected from the church. How can we use that to our advantage?

Paul himself says, "Knowledge puffs up, but love builds up" (1 Cor. 8:1). Jesus instructed us to, "have a childlike faith." To me nothing is more precious then the unquestioning simple faith of a child. Children ask innocent questions, obediently follow, and often remind us to pray. They say things like my six-year-old son recently said to me, "Daddy, we need to pray that God will get the boomerang out of the tree."

The boomerang was sixty feet up, wedged between two branches. So we prayed and to our amazement the boomerang was sitting on a branch where he could reach it a couple of hours later. As a result, we were able to praise God together for that answer to prayer. My son did not need more knowledge to believe or act upon that belief in prayer. Why is it that young ones like my son have this simple faith, only to grow distant from God as they move into their teenage years, in spite of all we have taught them?

Is doctrine bad? Are apologetics a problem? Is biblical world-view foolish? Not at all! These clearly target the mind of the believer with evidence and proof. These tools are great for young people who are ready and have an internal desire from the Lord to go deeper. Are they the answer for the kid sitting in a youth group engulfed in guilt and surrounded by friends who claim to know the Lord but invite him to parties, help him get there, and hide the act from his parents? Apologetics, worldview, and doctrine target the individual faith of a person, not the person's community. In the postmodern world the community, also called the body of Christ, impacts our young people today as greatly if not more than the truth.

Knowledge plays a pivotal role in our spiritual life. But is it the agent of change? If it were, would not knowing something immediately result in deep change within? This is frequently not the case. It is also true that we cannot change if we do not know the truth of Scripture. Once again we have the knowledge dilemma.

The knowledge dilemma raises the interesting question of how we balance knowledge growth and spiritual growth. Clearly one does not guarantee the other. We can see this in Paul's life, in the lives of our young people today, and probably in some of the adults we know within our churches.

As we have sought to decode the knowledge dilemma that we see at work in the dual lives of our young people, we have come to understand that students often believe knowledge to be the convicting agent of God. When knowledge is the convicting agent, students are pushed back under the Law. These students feel guilty all the time or grow numb to the feeling altogether.

The challenge today is that many of our youth know enough to live a close to perfect life. Just look back at the list of expectations they give in our sessions. Can they live up to what they know? It would be great if we could always be joyful, always see God's eternal plan, and always have strong faith. But that is not reality. Many of our shortcomings are used by God to draw us closer to Him and to bring us to an increasing understanding that apart from Him, we can do nothing. This is not the message our youth are receiving.

Jesus, being God, knew the path to seeing deep life change occur in His disciples. It was not knowledge and performance that would cause His disciples to wrestle deeply with their own motivations and the issues that arose from within. This moves us to understand why Jesus called himself the Good Shepherd.

CHAPTER EIGHT

THE GOOD SHEPHERD

---

*I*t is a warm summer afternoon The shepherd sits on a hill above his flock. Having been with the sheep all day, the warmth of the late afternoon sun threatens to lull the shepherd to sleep. As the sun sinks toward the horizon, shadows are cast across the valley. The shepherd could easily let his mind wander as the day draws to a close.

Safe in the valley below, sheep graze happily, growing more active as the cool of the shadows crosses the valley floor. The brilliance of the sky glows with deeper and deeper shades of orange and red upon the clouds. Shadows engulf the entire valley where the shepherd's flock grazes, unaware of any approaching danger. The shepherd knows that this is the worst time of the day to let down his guard.

The sheep trust their shepherd because he has faithfully protected them for years. His vigilance increases as dusk draws near because predators seek the cover of evening to make their advance on his flock in hopes of an easy meal. His pulse quickens as he scans the horizon looking for any movement so that he can move quickly to step in between his sheep and their enemy.

Today, many dangers assail our young people. So many obvious dangers are present in our culture that it is easy to become focused on them. This may lead us to overlook the more subtle risks such as the deceptive dual life that can just as quickly lead to the destruction of a flock.

On the Indian reservations of Arizona, entire flocks of sheep will be found at the bottom of a ravine, having willingly run off the cliff one after another. They ran head long after each other all the while believing they were heading in the best direction. Sheep, not being the brightest, are prone to follow the direction of those around them without thinking for themselves. This explains why, in a storm and without a shepherd, an entire flock can be found dashed on the rocks at the foot of a cliff.

The shepherds of these flocks failed to recognize the approach of a distant storm and were not in place to calm their sheep or go before them to lead them to safety. Today many youth groups are running head long into danger as the intentionally deceptive dual life becomes the predominant culture within the group. Many sheep are being led away from their shepherd and into some of the obvious dangers we are attempting to protect them from: alcohol, sex, and drugs. When we focus on the threats from outside the flock, it's easy to miss or turn a blind eye to the risk factors that can arise from *within* our own flock.

The dual life and the weight of the expectations many students carry are two internal risk factors we cannot afford to overlook. They are vital because we are ministering to postmodern teens who need to experience the truth in their lives and communities. When teens feel like they will never measure up to all we expect and find themselves in a community that is pulling them into a dual life, they can't see how they will ever experience the love, grace, and sanctifying power God can bring into their lives.

Examining the expectation lists church youth create reveals a focus on performance and behaviors. This calls into question our approach to leadership. And what we believe as leaders is important. Today the focus on leadership within our country and church is clear. We find seminars, books, tapes, and conferences devoted to the topic.

Looking into the definition of *lead* and *leader* we find:

Lead

1. To show the way to others, usually by going ahead of them
2. To be the route or direction that goes to a particular place or in a particular direction
3. To **control, direct, or command others**[15]

Leader

1. Somebody who guides or directs others or **by telling them how to behave**
2. Somebody or something in front of all others, for example, in a race or procession
3. The head of a nation, political party, legislative body, or military unit[16]

Misdirected Leadership

Today it is hard to find examples of leaders who lead by showing others the way. Rather, we witness a form of leadership in our companies and government entities that focuses on command and control. Often these commands and controls target the performance and or behavior of those they lead. This is especially true of leaders who work with our young people. It seems common practice to approach our teenagers with the mindset of controlling their behavior because we do not want them to get hurt. As a result, they often encounter a control-based approach at school, church, and at home.

Have we stopped to ask how Jesus viewed leadership? A look into the word *leader* in the Bible reveals that it appears only four times in the New Testament. Two of these references are found in Jesus' teaching, another is a reference to an Old Testament leader in Hebrews, and the fourth is referring to obeying one's leaders in the book of Hebrews.

Jesus' teaching regarding leadership is in direct contrast to what we witness in our culture today. In Matthew 23:6-10 and Luke 22:26 Jesus directly addressed the desire to lead:

Matt. 23:6-10:

> And they love the place of honor at banquets, and the chief seats at the synagogues, and respectful greetings in the market places, and being called leader by men, Rabbi. But do not be called Rabbi (leader); for One is your Teacher and you are all brothers.

Luke 22:25-26:

> The kings of the Gentiles lord it over them; and those who have authority over them are called Benefactors. But not so with you, but let him who is greatest among you become as the youngest and the leader as a servant.

Today, many people talk about servant leadership yet often the approach is still consistent with leading and directing others. In these verses, the reference to the greatest among you becoming as the youngest would indicate that there would be no way for that person as the youngest to direct the behavior of others.

Jesus' Approach

How do we reconcile Jesus' teaching with our preoccupation with leadership? Have we allowed our view of leadership to alter our understanding of Jesus' ministry?

Jesus and His disciples represent the most compelling ministry success of all time. His disciples, absent Judas, lived out their faith to the point of their deaths. They did this not through violent acts and seeking revenge, but by peacefully submitting to authority that sought to kill them for their teaching, for their faith. How did Jesus accomplish this significant life transformation in just three years with His disciples? Was His success based upon His strength, His authority, His ability to command and control His disciples' behavior?

Command and control were certainly within the realm of possibility for Jesus, being God! He could have conceivably forced anyone to do anything He wished. We do find that Jesus forced His will upon demons that possessed people, by casting them out. But we do not find a single example of Jesus forcing His will upon a person in control of his own faculties. Today teens tell us that they frequently find themselves under leadership that uses its power and authority to control their actions, behavior, and often their choice of activities.

We need to ask ourselves, how did Jesus view His role in the life of the disciples? Note how Jesus describes Himself in John 10:14:

> I am the good shepherd, and I know My own and My own know
> Me, even as the Father knows Me and I know the Father; and I lay
> down my life for the sheep.

Jesus referred to Himself as the Good Shepherd, not a great leader. Let me say that again, Jesus referred to Himself as the Good Shepherd, not a great leader. Yet within the Roman Empire, shepherds were not viewed as great leaders; that distinction was reserved for Caesar along with the senators and governors of Rome. In the synagogue the great leaders were none other than the Pharisees. Jesus viewed Himself as a shepherd, yet many today would say Jesus led the greatest movement in human history. This movement took Christianity from a rogue band of disciples and eventually converted the entire Roman Empire to Christianity.

The word shepherd is defined as:

1. Somebody who looks after sheep
2. Somebody who is responsible for caring for and guiding a group of people, especially a Christian minister
3. To look after sheep

4. To guide a group of people somewhere
5. To look after the well-being of a group of people[17]

Comparing the definitions of leadership and shepherd, we see that leadership is more about directing and outcome and less about care, well-being, and guiding. Shepherding is more about influence and less about behavior, more about the journey and less about performance, more about the desire of the sheep and less about control.

The expectations list we discussed in chapter four points to an outcome in the lives of our youth that would indicate we approach youth in a manner more consistent with leading rather than shepherding. The result of this approach is that our youth perceive that we are more about rules that aim to control; we are focused on their behavior rather than who they are and want to become. To them, this becomes all about performance. As a result, they often master the art of performing for us even though their hearts are far from God. Our sheep believe we are more about performance and behavior than about their care and well-being which are key attributes of a good shepherd.

As the Good Shepherd, Jesus modeled a form of leadership that was counter culture for His time. Jesus could have easily followed the leadership example of the day. Instead He sought disciples who desired to follow, showing them how to serve and sacrifice as opposed to *requiring* them to do so. This was a sharp break from the system and primary motivational style of the Old Testament, Law and sacrifice, which brought questions and condemnation from religious leaders. In this counter culture approach Jesus was so attractive that His disciples willingly followed, and so did crowds of thousands.

Why did so many desire to follow Jesus? The answer is found in Philippians 2:5-8, which confirms that Jesus' approach to ministry was not about authority and control.

Have this attitude in yourselves which was also in Christ Jesus,
who, although He existed in the form of God, did not regard equal-
ity with God a thing to be grasped, but emptied Himself, taking
the form of a bond-servant, and being made in the likeness of men.
And being found in appearance as a man, He humbled Himself by
becoming obedient to the point of death, even death on a cross.

Jesus, being God, did not count equality with God something to be grasped. Making Himself a bondservant, He laid down His life. Jesus' approach and demeanor were drastically different than the leaders of the synagogue and of Rome. They were so different that crowds of thousands followed Him from city to city, forcing Jesus to slip away. Jesus' non-authoritative, compassion-based approach to the disciples and masses was so attractive that they followed Him into situations many of us would seek to avoid today. Jesus truly cared about the well being of His flock. The result was that the disciples and crowds believed His message and desired to follow Him, not out of compulsion or externally driven expectations, but from an internal desire.

Jesus' example sets forth a number of timeless principles related to shepherding that resulted in the transformation of His disciples. This transformation is attested to by the disciples' internal desire to follow Jesus beyond His death and resurrection. Today 70 percent of our youth do not have an internal desire to continue to follow Jesus once they're out from under our control. In contrast, all of Jesus' disciples except Judas went on to lay down their lives. They willingly protected the progress that had been made with their flocks of young believers as a result of His ministry in their lives.

Timeless Principles of Shepherding
- A good shepherd does not see himself as a leader.
- A good shepherd takes ownership.

- A good shepherd takes responsibility for his sheep.
- A good shepherd goes before his sheep.
- A good shepherd trusts his sheep.

A Good Shepherd Does Not See Himself as a Leader

Jesus chose to shepherd His disciples rather than lead them. Shepherding implies more care of and for the sheep rather than directing to a desired outcome or behavior. When Jesus called the disciples, He did so not with an impassioned speech filled with warning and conviction. He did not use a rallying cry for or against a significant cause. Jesus simply said, "Follow me."

To a leader, this would seem like an ineffective way to assemble a team or to lead the charge. When Jesus said follow Me, each individual had a choice. Do I want to follow Him?

Their decision to follow was not based upon some vision, cause, or even guilt trip, but something deeper, more genuine, and infinitely more attractive. Being God, Jesus had an inherent humility, sacrificial nature, genuine care, and compassion for His people that was compelling. Jesus did not have a long list of expectations the disciples needed to meet to win His favor. Paul echoes this approach in Ephesians 2:8-9.

> For by grace you have been saved through faith; and that not of yourselves, it is the gift of God; not as a result of works, so that no one may boast.

Jesus' genuine care was in stark contrast to the Pharisees, the spiritual leaders of the day.

It was the Pharisees who Jesus called "whitewashed tombs" because they were both far from God and far from genuine compassion for their flock. They sought the performance of the sheep in added rituals, sacrifices, and temple taxes. This led them to, in the words of Jesus, turn the temple courts into a den of thieves who preyed upon the Pharisees' own flock. In Jesus the disciples did not find the "wise" guile of crafty leaders who had the latest motivational technique or game to move His followers. They found genuine love and care.

Examining discipleship

Today, many talk about discipleship and seek to disciple rather than be a shepherd. In fact, the word *discipler* does not exist in Greek or English. Rather the model we find in the Gospels is that Jesus, the Good Shepherd, had disciples. This realization significantly alters the nature, purpose, and goals of a discipleship relationship. A shepherd is focused on care, well-being, and going before rather than on teaching and applying instruction to the lives of his disciples. The Shepherd seeks something deeper to occur within His sheep, something that wells up from within that brings about deep and lasting life change.

It is clear by the manner in which Jesus called the disciples that they choose to follow Him of their own volition. In fact, three of the disciples decided to follow Jesus prior to even being called by Him.

Andrew, John 1:40:

> *One of the two who heard John speak, and followed Him, was Andrew Simon Peter's brother.*

Simon, John 1:41-42:

> *He found first his own brother, Simon, and said to him, "We have found the Messiah." He brought him to Jesus. Jesus looked at him, and said, "You are Simon the son of John: you shall be called Cephas.*

Nathanael, John 1:45:

> *Philip found Nathanael and said to him, "We have found Him of whom Moses in the Law and also the Prophets wrote, Jesus of Nazareth, the son of Joseph."*

Jesus was their Shepherd because they chose to follow Him. This was the catalyst for deep life change in His young disciples. Previously they had been required to perform the Law. Under Jesus they had freedom from the Law and developed the desire to follow and see their life change over time.

Jesus saw Himself as a Shepherd, not simply a Teacher. He led His followers out of the temple and into the streets among the masses just as a shepherd takes his sheep out of the pen and into the valley to graze. Taking His disciples out of the classroom environment of the synagogue where knowledge was taught and the Torah was debated represented a radical departure in the teaching style of the day.

Jesus knew that it would be among the masses that He could go before His disciples showing them the way, as a shepherd does with his flock. While the shepherd understands that there is inherently more danger in the mountains than in the pen, he doesn't allow that fact to keep him from doing what is healthiest and best for his sheep. The Good Shepherd knew that in the midst of increased danger there came a sense of increased freedom in the valley. Taking them out of the pen allowed His sheep to explore the valley where they encountered real people and challenges. They were confronted with their own thoughts that would seek to judge many of the people with whom they came in contact.

Jesus did this because He would be there to help them as needed. He would be there for them as they wrestled with real life in a real valley filled with real danger. As a result, His sheep developed a desire, based upon real reasons and experiences, to follow the voice of their Shepherd.

Jesus knew that His disciples would grow to truly understand what it meant to love and serve the unlovable only if they were out among them. It was in the context of *experience* and being confronted with their own desire to judge that they were forced to grapple deeply with their own motivations. We know Jesus saw the masses and had compassion upon them, not disdain. He saw them as if they were sheep without a shepherd. What is amazing is that Jesus took men, as ordinary as you and me, and changed their focus. They went from merely surviving in a difficult pre-modern culture to having compassion for and sacrificing for the Samaritan woman, the prostitute, the leper, the tax collector, the doctor, and the Pharisee as seen in the transformation of Paul! In the freedom and grace of Christ, they grew in their own desire to love, have compassion, and sacrifice for the hurting, sick, and oppressed.

This was accomplished because Jesus did not treat the disciples like they were His to control. Jesus knew that control would only work as long as He was there to exert control over them. Jesus, unlike the Pharisees who would always be around to try to control others' behavior, knew that He would leave the disciples in just a few short years. This necessitated a different approach. He looked to the future, seeking to develop the hearts of the disciples so that they would want to follow the faith, serve, and sacrifice of their own volition. We as parents and youth ministry leaders face the same reality. Our teens will not always be in our care.

In just three short years Jesus saw these men transformed into shepherds of the first century church, a church that saw 3,000 come to faith in just the first day of their ministry. The church created by these shepherds was unique. Individuals sold property to take care of one another, creating a safe place where people felt cared for. This was critical for the success of the church in that culture. The church was so attractive in terms of what was taught and how they lived that new believers would be disowned by their families for believing in Christ. Yet they walked confidently and safely into a community that would care for them.

How did Jesus infuse His love of the masses into the disciples? Jesus took upon Himself a position that would have been viewed by many in the culture as the lowest form of leadership, a shepherd. In this role Jesus sought not to lead but to give care. Through this humble approach He transformed not just the minds, but also the hearts of His disciples.

A Good Shepherd Takes Ownership

It is easy to discern the mindset of a shepherd. Does he view the sheep as his own, or does he see himself only as their hired hand? Jesus, the Good Shepherd, did not identify shepherds by their leadership skills, their position in life, or their abilities, but rather the perspective they took regarding their flock.

Many wealthy men in the Roman Empire hired shepherds to tend their flocks. As is the case today, it was often difficult to find good help, especially help that would truly care for their flocks. Jesus spoke to this challenge in John 10:11-15

> I am the good shepherd; The good shepherd lays down His life for
> the sheep. He who is a hireling, and not a shepherd, who is not the
> owner of the sheep, beholds the wolf coming, and leaves the sheep,
> and flees, and the wolf snatches them, and scatters them. He flees
> because he is a hireling and is not concerned about the sheep. I
> am the good shepherd, and I know my own and my own know me,
> even as the Father knows me and I know the Father; and I lay
> down My life for the sheep.

Today we find great frustration among youth ministry leaders across the country because many truly do care about their sheep, but they are frequently undermined by the messages their churches and often parents unintentionally send, discrediting their efforts in their students' lives. Today some parents leave the shepherding of their flock up to hired hands, believing that they have done all they can.

From John 10:11-15, we see that Jesus was not thrilled by the perspective of the religious leaders of His day. They approached the sheep with the attitude of mere hired hands. Jesus set a wholly different example, an example that valued His sheep as His own. A shepherd-owner was keenly concerned with the sheep's well-being because the shepherd's future was 100 percent dependent upon his flock's staying healthy. It was his flock that provided the shepherd and his family with the wool that became their clothing and served as the economic engine for their well-being. Losing just one sheep was a great blow. In many ways, the owner's well-being and that of his family were directly tied to the well-being, health, and safety of his sheep.

A good shepherd understood that allowing even one sheep to be wounded haphazardly would mean more time away from his flock. While he tended the one wounded sheep, more sheep were open to attack. This could create a spiral that could destroy His flock and, subsequently, his family. Danger did not lead Jesus to keep His disciples safe in the pen of the synagogue. Instead He took them out among the masses where there was significant danger. Jesus trusted that He and God, the Father, could protect them.

Our Approach Today

Today many parents are taking upon themselves the responsibility for leading and educating their children and teens, partly due to a growing fear of the culture in which we live. It's easy for parents and ministry leaders to grow so fearful of the failure and harm that can come to their sheep that they conclude it's best to keep them safe in the pen. As a result, the sheep do not encounter the dangerous world where they come to understand the need or develop the desire to follow their shepherds: their parents, ministry leaders, and ultimately their Good Shepherd in heaven. Our fear of what might happen can easily keep us from doing the very things Jesus did with His disciples. It is sometimes difficult to trust the Father in heaven to protect our young ones, especially if we, as teens, made mistakes and were hurt. As we look throughout the Bible, we find many examples of how fear leads to poor decisions. Think about Jonah's fear of going to Nineveh and the army of Israel's fear of Goliath. We also find direct teaching that indicates we are to fear nothing, but instead trust God.

Jesus, as the owner of His sheep, knew them intimately. The relationship ran deep between Him and His disciples, given all the time they spent traveling on foot from town to town. Today, our culture tells us it is difficult if not impossible to have a good relationship with our teens; however, from our discussions with teens, we do not believe this to be the case. Instead, we find they desire real involvement in their lives from their parents, but not the type of behavior-driven control they frequently experience. In truth, they desire to have a shepherd rather than a parent. They desire a shepherd who they can come to when challenges and questions arise in order to receive help, not a lecture.

Jesus placed His sheep above the masses because He knew that they would reach unbelievers after His ascension. In fact, if one analyzes the time Jesus spent with the disciples in comparison to that which He spent with the unsaved, His priority is clear.

Jesus would do anything to go before His followers so they might desire to serve their flocks when He departed from them. His love and care for the well-being of His sheep meant that when the wolves came seeking to scatter and devour the flock, He would confront them directly. Ultimately, He would peacefully lay down His life for them. He would not discredit His message of a loving, gracious God who desired a real relationship with them.

Jesus didn't opt to just feed the sheep in the pen where there was no danger and less work. Instead, He focused on taking them out into the world. Amid the danger and attacks of the religious leaders, Jesus developed sheep that felt loved, cared for, and safe.

Even more amazing, the disciples rose above the temptation of the world under this approach, inspite of attending gatherings with their Shepherd that led some to accuse Jesus of being a drunkard. It was in the care of their Shepherd out in the world that the disciples grew to love not only their Shepherd, but also the masses of sinful people around them.

A Good Shepherd Takes Responsibility for His Sheep

Andrew and Simon Peter represent an example of Jesus' shepherd-ing heart. A shepherd knows that he is 100 percent responsible for the safety, direction, and destination of the flock. It is he who leads them from field to field and gets them to their destination. Jesus did so with an open hand. He did not designate every step; He opened an entire valley floor for them to explore! We see an example of this in the lives of Andrew and Peter who decided to follow Jesus of their own volition.

John 1:35-36, 40-41 says:

> *Again the next day John was standing with two of his disciples, and he looked upon Jesus as He walked, and said, "Behold, the Lamb of God!"... One of the two who heard John speak, and followed Him, was Andrew, Simon Peter's brother. He found first his own brother Simon and said to him, "We have found the Messiah."*

Andrew decided to follow Jesus not based upon Jesus' calling Him, but because John the Baptist declared that Jesus was the Lamb of God. In His excitement Andrew went and found his brother Simon Peter. Together they decided to follow Jesus, even before Jesus gathered His group of disciples and began His itinerant ministry.

When Jesus was ready to launch His journey with His disci-ples, He sought out Andrew and Simon Peter in a boat fishing. It was at this point that Jesus issued the famous call to both Andrew and Simon Peter.

Mark 1:16-17:

> *As He was going along by the Sea of Galilee, He saw Simon and Andrew, the brother of Simon, casting a net in the sea; for they*

were fishermen. And Jesus said to them, "Follow Me, and I will
make you become fishers of men." And they immediately left their
nets and followed Him.

This is the only call where Jesus added, "I will make you
become fishers of men." The rest of the disciples either decided
to follow because they knew of Jesus or because He invited them,
"Follow Me."

When asked about this passage, many of our youth perceive
this call to be an expectation requiring them to become a fisher
of men. It is one of the many expectations they have been taught.
Yet reaching non-Christian friends is frequently in direct contra-
diction to other messages we send them like, "Don't hang out
with sinful people." They rightly ask, "How does that work?" Our
contradictions discredit our teaching and the faith in our desire to
protect our sheep from ungodly people.

We find throughout the gospels that Jesus and His disciples
regularly hung out with sinful people and they did not fall into heinous sin. Jesus even took His disciples to parties where they were
among people who were getting drunk, and yet they did not fall!

As I look to developing the teenagers in my own home, it is
this type of teen I desire to have, one who can stand in the face
of sin and bring glory to God! How did Jesus accomplish this?
He took responsibility for outcomes in the lives of His disciples
instead of setting requirements and expectations they needed to
perform. He also did not blame them when they fell short.

Look back at Mark 1:16-17, where Jesus calls Simon and
Andrew to follow Him. To understand Jesus' principle, one needs
to identify the active agent in this verse. Jesus says, "I will make
you." Jesus was taking responsibility for this outcome. It is a
promise, not an expectation. If the disciples **did not** become fishers of men, it is Jesus who would have been seen as the failure,
not the disciples.

Today it seems that parents and ministry leaders have come to see themselves as leaders directing and working to control the behavior of their sheep. In this model it becomes easy to blame the sheep when they fall short of our expectations. Given the list of expectations our youth find themselves under from society, the church, and home, it is inevitable that they will fall short. They are imperfect and will be so throughout their lives. Sanctification is a life-long process. Grace came to the disciples not through a long list of expectations and spotless performance, but through a loving Shepherd that knew His sheep were dumb and prone to fail. He took upon Himself not only their sin but also the responsibility for the outcome of their lives.

What would it mean to our young people if we, as parents and leaders, took responsibility for the shortcomings in their faith and lives? What if, instead of a harsh voice to convict or consequences to sanctify our teens, we sat humbly with them and asked questions like, "How do you feel about what just happened?" What if we set aside our need to be right and show them where they are wrong, and instead we conversed with them about life? What if we laid down our lives for them and repented of our shortcomings as parents and leaders? Would our teens sense a good shepherd in their lives? As shepherds, we should be on our knees repenting for the outcome we have allowed in our flocks.

A Good Shepherd Goes Before His Sheep

We have already discussed the fact that Jesus led His sheep out of the pen and went before them among the masses. This was essential in His approach to His followers because it meant they truly had to have the desire to follow Him. Once no longer in the pen, they could easily hang back and disappear into the crowd. Today many of our youth are held in the pen for their whole lives. When released from the pen as they leave our homes, they often cannot handle the freedom. In response to being held in the pen, high school students have devised a way to hang back and escape in the form of the dual lives seen within many of our youth ministries.

Internal Desire

How did Jesus create a desire within the hearts of His disciples to follow Him in a harsh world and an environment of spiritual leaders who had disillusioned many of His people? The secret to Jesus' success is found not in deep biblical teaching or convicting messages but in a simple verse found in John 10:1-5.

> Truly, truly I say to you, he who does not enter by the door into the fold of the sheep, but climbs up some other way, he is a thief and a robber. But he who enters by the door is a shepherd of the sheep. To him the doorkeeper opens, and the sheep hear his voice, and he calls his own sheep by name and leads them out. When he puts forth all his own, he goes before them, and the sheep follow him because they know his voice. **A stranger they simply will not follow,** but will flee from him, because they do not know the voice of strangers (emphasis added).

The close of this passage speaks to the heart of every parent and ministry leader when it says, a stranger's voice they simply will not follow. Isn't that our deepest desire? Is it not our hope that our kids will follow our voices and ultimately the Holy Spirit's leading rather than a stranger's voice?

This passage would indicate that the owner of the sheep has the ability to call his sheep out by name. They will follow him even when in a pen with sheep from other shepherds. It does not indicate that there was no contact between his sheep and the sheep of the world. The disciples were often with the sheep of the world and did not fall or stray because their relationship was so strong with their Shepherd. They followed His voice even in tempting environments. Jesus could simply call to them and they responded out of desire. They separated themselves from the others of their own volition. They did so not because of external expectations or fear of the Shepherd's staff in the form of consequences or punishment, but out of a genuine desire to follow. Today it seems that our Christian culture tells us that consequences or punishment are the best way to train a teen, yet our interviews with teens support what is taught in 1 John 4:18.

> There is no fear in love; but perfect love casts out fear, because fear involves punishment and the one who fears is not perfected in love.

This passage sits in contrast to the saying, 'spare the rod, spoil the child,' which does not indicate where childhood ends. In biblical times, teens were getting married anywhere between the ages of thirteen to sixteen, but today we often approach teens like they are still young children. Why are we then surprised that in return we often receive child-like behavior?

What Voice Do Teens Follow Today?

As we interact with teens across the country, we find that many are open to or are already following a stranger's voice because they do not have a deep relationship with the shepherds in their lives. Not sensing belief or trust, many are ready to abandon the leadership of their parents and even ministry leaders.

Youth who feel controlled and required to follow instead of shepherded are frequently checked out on their faith. They feel they are frequently approached by strong voices and threats of punishment. Many parents believe this is the only way to train teens to do what is right and avoid sin in a fast-paced, busy world. Indeed it is hard to take the time needed to maintain a real relationship with their teens. It is even harder to go before them in a world that has drawn so many lines between parents and teens. It is far faster and easier to punish teens than to go before them and shepherd with a voice they will want to follow.

Students who feel they are approached in a performance-based manner are often ready to follow a stranger's voice in high school ... any stranger's voice. Frequently the stranger's voice they follow is a boyfriend's or girlfriend's or a peer's within their own youth ministry! Together these sheep have found voices outside the church that seem more willing to accept their shortcomings and let them explore the valley. As a result, they are often running head long toward a cliff like the sheep frightened in a storm with no shepherd to guide them to safety.

Students often find themselves dependent upon each other for guidance because they have tuned out their shepherd's voice. As shepherds of teens, we need to recognize that our time with our sheep is drawing to a close. We need to prepare them to live in the world without falling. By the time our sheep leave our homes and youth ministries they need to have developed the desire to follow the voice of the Lord in their lives, not because they have to but because they want to.

There is one simple reason for this. Once they leave our homes and enter the world we will no longer be there to check on what they're doing. No longer will the staff be present in the form of a curfew, confiscating car keys, or removing privileges to make them walk the straight and narrow. Our teens need to have the desire to do what is right apart from our ability to bring consequences into their lives.

Would it not be far better as a shepherd to have such a relationship with our teens that they still desire to please us, not because we can punish them, but because they know they are loved, believed in, and trusted? Would it not be better for us to have the platform for them to turn to us when they face challenges and fall because they know they will be cared for and restored to health in our loving gracious arms?

A Good Shepherd Trusts His Sheep

One of the more challenging roles of a shepherd is trusting sheep that are inherently not trustworthy. Even more difficult for a shepherd is trusting those who have already fallen short and failed. Sheep, by their nature, are easily distracted and prone to get themselves into trouble. We would prefer to have them earn our trust before we extend any real responsibility. Can sheep ever earn the trust of a shepherd? Looking to the sheep to earn trust lends itself to an inherently performance-based approach: "If you perform and prove yourself, then I will trust you."

Trust is hard to come by in our culture. Too often we have been let down or hurt by people close to us, even by spiritual leaders we have admired. However, we find in Paul's teaching on love a statement about the nature of love which says love always trusts or believes all things! (1 Cor. 13:7)

Having been hurt by people I trusted, this verse troubled me. I raised the question of love always trusting with a senior pastor whom I have known for many years. His response to my wrestling with this passage was to say trust is earned. He gave a convincing argument for why we did not need to inherently trust people in the world and even within the church. His arguments left me with several critical questions.

1. *Can anyone earn our trust?*

We are all sinful people, products of living in a fallen world. We are prone to make mistakes, say stupid things, and let people down. How many of us have hurt someone close to us? Clearly we want to be trustworthy as individuals. We also are looking to leaders of the church to be people of good reputation; but none of us is perfect, including our young people.

2. *Can we earn the trust of God in our fallen state?*

Examining the hall of faith in Hebrews, we find many great men who we know failed including Abraham, Moses, and David, who was called a man after God's own heart.[18] Because of their failure, people were hurt and even killed. Trust was broken. Should we conclude that God can trust no one? If He can trust no one then neither can we! Both Abraham and Moses committed murder, yet they were given greater responsibility based upon a proper heart response to their failures. Think that through. God was quick to trust them again in spite of their failures.

Paul teaches that love believes all things! As a Pharisee, Paul himself was charged with leading people according to the will of God. In his pursuit of the Law and righteousness, he missed the Messiah entirely and persecuted Christians until he met the Lord on the road to Damascus. Paul had failed God in devastating ways yet God still called him to reach the Gentiles! Eventually, Paul went on to compose one of the most powerful passages regarding the nature of love.

Jesus modeled with His disciples the unwarranted trust that Paul teaches in 1 Corinthians. Shortly after calling His disciples to follow Him, Jesus assigned them vital roles that were central to carrying out the ministry as they traveled from city to city. The Good Shepherd understood that apart from genuine trust, the disciples would not feel loved. He knew they would respond to that love with an internal desire to follow, serve, and love those around them. He trusted them even though they, like sheep, were prone to make mistakes.

Jesus modeled this amazing form of trusting love even though He knew all the disciples would betray him upon His arrest, running and hiding in fear. He knew that Peter would deny Him three times. He even put Judas in charge of the money knowing that he would eventually betray Him for a bag of silver. God regularly bestows responsibility upon us in spite of our propensity to fail and disappoint Him.

In our time with young people we have found that they rarely perceive they are believed in and trusted. Instead, they feel like they are falling short of our expectations. This causes them to hide their failures from us for fear of condemnation and consequences. What would happen if we believed what Paul said in Romans 8:1-2:

> *There is therefore now no condemnation for those who are in*
> *Christ Jesus. For the law of the Spirit of life in Christ Jesus has set*
> *you free from the law of sin and of death.*

Belief and trust are powerful agents and in many ways serve as the foundation of genuine love. Apart from genuine trust, the foundation for love is shaky. One is always open to being doubted and questioned which places them under a performance standard. When belief and trust are extended by a loving shepherd who is more concerned about the well-being of his sheep than their performance, the sheep respond in kind with love for those around them.

In business, a manager who believes and trusts his employees often finds that they rise to that belief and trust. Those who are concerned about their employee's performance and behavior often micro-manage; they don't extend trust. In such an environment, people often have low morale because they do not perceive that they are trusted. As a result, they tend to under perform, be more unruly, and make excuses.

Do We Trust Our Teens?

When interacting with teens I often hear that they want to be believed in and trusted. Some parents respond by saying, "But they are not trustworthy." Are we as parents truly trustworthy before God? Apparently He extends us trust by giving us children to nurture and assigning us to be His ambassadors to carry out His ministry on earth. When people are treated as if they are trustworthy they typically become more so.

When our youth sense that the world has a negative view of them and that we do not believe or trust that they can avoid sin and serve God in meaningful ways, they lose a powerful motivator to avoid sin and serve the King. Trusting unworthy sheep is at the bedrock of God's love for us. This type of love needs to be extended to young people. Like Jesus, we might be surprised to see them exceed our hopes when we seek to be good shepherds in their lives.

We faced this exact situation with one of my disciples who was in many ways an adopted son. Larry's story spans ten years and is fraught with disappointment and betrayal. But ultimately, there's victory.

Larry was a young man full of potential but with a hole at the bottom of his heart. It was impossible to fill up his insatiable need for approval, acceptance, and attention. When we first met him he was in high school and a nonbeliever. As the years passed, he accepted Christ and became a consistent part of Deedee's and my life. Not long after meeting him it became clear that the hole in his heart made him untrustworthy, not because he was a bad person but because he would say what he needed to say to get the approval and love of whomever he was with. Frequently what he said was not what he really meant or planned to do. His words were true the second he said them but a few minutes later in front of someone else, they could quickly be countermanded which resulted in many lies.

When his problem became clear to us, we had a decision to make. Should we attack his sin of lying, likely pushing him away from being one of our disciples, or should we choose to trust him? Should we serve him and love him in spite of the glaring issue that often backfired and hurt us time and time again? While we wanted to immediately confront his sin, we also knew that he would not change quickly, given the depth of his hurt. And we knew his hurt was ongoing due to his family environment.

We all carry areas of woundedness. Wounds heal over time and require treatment, care, and a measure of tenderness. While this is readily apparent with physical wounds, when it comes to deeper emotional wounds we as believers often have a callous, uncaring approach. We want people to just trust God and get over it.

In spite of the obvious risks and challenges we chose to trust Larry. We invited him into the inner circle of our lives and ministry. The fruit of our approach that repeatedly extended love, grace, and trust became evident when He began calling me Dad.

Our approach created a dilemma within Larry. He knew he was not trustworthy but he loved the feeling of being trusted. In spite of his desire to be worthy of our trust, there were frequent situations in which he deliberately misled us. At one point he even committed a financial fraud that was large enough to be considered a felony. At that point, we had been walking alongside Larry for almost eight years. We directly confronted his deceit. He admitted his wrongdoing and made restitution for it over time. Because we continued to invest in his life even after a major failure, he finally began to be truly transformed as the Holy Spirit convicted him and changed his heart.

Larry's involvement with a national grace-based training ministry, our discipleship, and consistent grace and love bore significant fruit in his life. Recently we visited him in his home with his lovely wife and twelve-week-old baby. He is growing to be a godly man others can rely on. If anyone could have ended up as a con man on the wrong side of the tracks, it was Larry. Today he is developing a character based upon a sound relationship with the Lord who loves him in spite of his hurt and failings. As shepherds in his life we modeled a belief and trust he had never encountered. That repeated grace and unwarranted belief and trust was a cornerstone in his life that called him powerfully to the way he should go.

The first youth ministry in our country, Christian Endeavor, operated on this principle. This ministry, founded by a twenty-six-year-old college graduate, grew to have a national presence in just a few short years.[19] The base principle of Christian Endeavor was that nothing should be done for a teen that they could do for themselves. As a result, the youth ministry was run by students. They did everything at their weekly meeting from teaching to providing the food. The minimal adult leadership, normally one or two parents, sat in the back of the room serving only as advisors and equippers, helping those who desired to teach to prepare their talks. Under this approach the ministry grew to include 70,000 chapters in the United States.

In these ministries students were believed in, trusted, and empowered to do the mission and service projects they wanted. They often tackled projects that adults would have thought unlikely. In a period of poverty and racial unrest in the south, these youth ministries met with city leaders to discuss issues and to bring their youthful vigor to serve their communities. Many of the leaders we count as amazing men of God were raised up under this approach to ministry, including Billy Graham!

As the Good Shepherd, Jesus trusted and believed in His young disciples transforming their lives into the shepherds of the first century church. In John 14:12 He told them:

> *Truly, truly, I say to you, he who believes in Me, the works that I do, he shall do also; and **greater works than these he will do**; because I go to the Father. And whatever you ask in My name, that will I do, so that the Father may be glorified in the Son. If you ask Me anything in My name, I will do it (emphasis added).*

Our teens deserve the same type of unwarranted belief and trust today. Jesus turned the responsibility of shepherding His flock over to His disciples when He issued them the Great Commission to go and make disciples of all nations. He has bestowed the same challenge and privilege upon us as parents and ministry leaders today.

Our fast paced, get-it-done-yesterday culture has altered the art of shepherding today. In this environment it is far easier and more expedient to focus on the performance of our sheep with rewards and consequences than it is to take the approach of the Good Shepherd.

As the Good Shepherd, Jesus did not see Himself as a leader but humbled Himself, not seeking equality with God. In His humility He took on the role of a shepherd who led by His voice, not by His authority or powers of persuasion. Jesus took ownership of the sheep, understanding that they were vital to the success of the church after His departure.

As their owner Jesus took full responsibility for the outcomes in the lives of His sheep saying, "I will make you fishers of men." He did so knowing that if at the end of His time with His disciples they did not have the internal desire to continue as fishers of men, the failure would be upon the Shepherd, not the sheep. Jesus developed their internal desire by leading His sheep out of the pen and into the dangerous world where they would need to live and minister upon His departure. He knew that they would learn through experience in this difficult world and the benefit would be the wisdom of pursuing what is right, true, and holy.

Jesus also knew that people flourish when they are believed in and trusted by their shepherd and given real responsibility with real affects both positive and negative, if they succeeded or failed. Jesus knew that even though the disciples would scatter in fear upon His arrest, His laying down of authority and power for them would make all the difference. When Jesus returned from the dead He did so not with a harsh voice or condemnation for the disciples' weak faith and failure. Rather He returned with encouragement and grace. He even allowed doubting Thomas, who refused to believe, to put his fingers in His side in order to encourage Thomas back onto the playing field. Thomas the doubter was spurred on to love and good deeds! Only a few short days after their failure Jesus bestowed upon His disciples the Great Commission knowing that they would rise to the belief, trust, grace, and love that the God of the universe had bestowed upon them. After all, He was the Good Shepherd. Are we?

QUESTIONS AND REFLECTIONS

Questions for Parents and Leaders

What are the differences between shepherding and leading?

What words would the teens in your life use to describe you?

What do you think it would look like if you were to "go before" your teen in your home or ministry?

How would you rate the relationship between you and your teen? More importantly, how would your teen rate the relationship when they were talking with a friend?

What would your teens like to see change in your relationship with them?

Does fear play a role in the approach you take with your teen? If so, how?

Do your teens sense condemnation when they fall short? How and why?

Who's voice is your teen following today and why?

Do your sheep *desire* to follow your voice or do they feel they *have to* follow your voice?

Questions to ask your teen?

If you choose to ask these questions it is imperative that you do not disagree, correct or make excuses. When a parent or leader asks real questions, listens, and apologizes, if necessary, then reflects upon their sheep's perspective it always bears fruit. These questions can begin to build a platform for your voice in their lives.

Do you know without a doubt that I love you?

Do I care more about who you are or how you perform?

Do you believe I will be there for you no matter what?

How would you rate our relationship in terms of being honest and transparent on a scale of 1 to 10?

Do you know how to deal with guilt when you fail?

Would you come to me if you made a major mistake and were feeling guilty? Why or why not?

Follow Whom?

*I*t was an evening like any other evening until George, a student in our college ministry, called and asked to meet with me. When he arrived at our home he wanted to talk outside, tripping my internal alarms. As we stood by his truck, it became clear that the issue was even larger than I had perceived. George kept starting and stopping like a vehicle running out of fuel. Finally in one last spurt of courage he disclosed that he had attempted suicide. George was twenty-two, working and attending some college classes. He had been raised in the church and had at times served and walked closely with God. He had struggled the past couple of years, being out on his own feeling lonely and disconnected from the church.

As we talked, I realized that the guilt he felt due to pornography had taken a significant toll. This along with other issues in his life led him to believe he was useless to God and the church. He had been a leader in his youth group and had gone on several mission trips. Now he felt like his existence was futile. George believed God was not pleased with him and he should just end his suffering.

Six months earlier George and two other young men in our college ministry had disclosed an issue with pornography. For us this was a positive sign that things were beginning to happen in our ministry. Students were getting honest. Their honesty served to encourage us, given the obvious dual lives of many of the students involved in our group.

Meeting with each of them one-on-one resulted in three different approaches to their problem of pornography. George was so convicted that he actually sold his computer. Another asked me to put Internet protection software on his computer, which I did. The third had me call him every night at 10:00.

We began memorizing verses related to lust, keeping the marriage bed pure, and how precious young women were in the eyes of the Lord. Each week we talked and prayed together. Yet these practices combined with the accountability they requested seemed to be making only a minor difference. In spite of all the prayer, Scripture, and accountability, they all were still deeply entangled in pornography. Although the Internet had been disabled for two of them, they moved to other forms of pornography.

Within two weeks of George's attempted suicide, another of my three disciples struggling with pornography attempted suicide. My alarm was understandable and so were my questions. We had been working together for more than a year and had seen no dramatic change. Their frustration and discouragement at not seeing lasting victory increased to the point of despair. In spite of all the time I spent with them I had no idea that their discouragement had grown so deep.

The pain of these events for them and for me opened new levels of discussion and thought. All three had accepted the Lord as their Savior. They also knew the activities they were involved in were wrong and felt guilty because of them. In spite of all we had done, life transformation had eluded them. Their sense of guilt and shame had led to hopelessness. What was not clear to us was why there had been no lasting change.

We discussed their situations and studied the role of the Holy Spirit in believers' lives. Then we saw that the Holy Spirit was not behind the conviction two of them felt related to pornography. Instead, their self-imposed guilt and conviction seemed to stem from other sources. Those included: my discipling, others' teaching, the knowledge of good and evil, right and wrong, and the heinous view of sexual sin. The source had not been the Spirit pressing upon their souls, but rather *an intellectual belief that it was wrong based upon sound arguments presented in teaching.*

As we talked through events in each of their lives, we realized that the Holy Spirit had other issues He wanted to address with each of them. The Holy Spirit wanted to accomplish different types of life change in them at this time. This was a surprising revelation. As their leader, I had never stopped to consider the possibility that the timing of the sanctification process was different for each one of them. Nor had I considered that when they disclosed sin and guilt that the source might not be the Holy Spirit, but rather a message, knowledge, or even expectations placed upon them by others or even me.

I had overlooked the simple fact that people can feel guilty for many things and that guilt does not always arise from the conviction of the Holy Spirit. My failure to seek His sanctification process in the lives of these young men nearly cost two lives. Each of them had been attempting to change an obvious sin apart from the power of the Spirit that was fully needed to circumcise their hearts as described in Romans 2:29.

> *But he is a Jew who is one inwardly; and circumcision is that which is of the heart, by the Spirit, not by the letter; and his praise is not from men, but from God.*

Their efforts proved futile apart from the sanctification agent, the Holy Spirit. Today it seems that youth frequently hear messages regarding following Jesus and rarely hear messages related to the role of the Holy Spirit in their lives.

Setting Them Up To Succeed

If we look deeper into Jesus' ministry with the disciples we find that His message changed markedly as He neared the end of his time among them. It was potentially nine months to a year before being arrested in Gethsemane that Jesus began telling His disciples that He would not be with them much longer.

His message in John 13:33 is particularly enlightening.

Little children, I am with you a little while longer. You shall seek Me, and as I said to the Jews, I now say to you also, 'Where I am going, you cannot come.'

This type of message appeared more and more frequently as the Garden of Gethsemane and the cross drew closer. The disciples probably felt concerned and dismayed, and wondered what was next. In His infinite wisdom and love, Jesus began preparing them for His absence so they would continue His mission on earth beyond His direct involvement in their lives.

To prepare them, Jesus changed His message from "Follow Me" to "Where I am going you cannot follow!" This troubled the disciples who had walked intimately with and depended upon the Lord for more than three years. It also calls into question the message we send to young people today, that they should "Follow Jesus."

Jesus goes on to express incredible belief and trust in those disciples, saying in John 14:12:

Truly, truly, I say to you, he who believes in Me the works that I do he shall do also; and greater works than these shall he do, because I go to the Father.

Jesus expressed trust in the disciples knowing that they would shortly desert Him upon His arrest. He credits His belief in His followers to do greater works than He to His confidence in the One whom He will send to be their counselor. He explains this in John 14:15-17:

If you love me you will keep my commandments. And I will ask the Father, and He will give you another Helper that He may be with you forever, that is the Spirit of truth…

Jesus teaches the disciples that the Helper will be with them forever, guiding them in His absence. What an amazing picture. Jesus knows that if He stays among them they will follow Him. Their outreach would be limited because they would all have to be present with Jesus to hear His guidance. By giving the role of shepherd and guide to the indwelling power of the Spirit, Jesus enabled His disciples to go forth in different directions. This greatly expanded the impact and reach of His message of love and grace.

The Role of the Holy Spirit

Jesus was confident they could do great things because of His intimate knowledge of the power of the Holy Spirit to guide, sanctify, and strengthen them in His absence. During His final teaching time, He also taught the disciples some of the key roles the Holy Spirit would play in their lives.

John 14:17 the Spirit of Truth who abides with you and is in you.

John 14:26 the Holy Spirit whom the Father will send in My name, He will teach you all things and bring to remembrance all that I said to you.

John 15:26 the Spirit will bear witness of Me.

John 16:7 It is to your advantage that I go away for if I do not go away the Helper shall not come.

John 16:8 When He comes He (the Spirit) will convict the world concerning sin and righteousness.

John 16:13 But when the Spirit comes He will guide you into all truth.

It would be to their advantage for Jesus to leave them and for the Helper to come.

Teens and the Holy Spirit

Today it seems that our teens know little of the life-transforming power of the Helper Jesus sent to guide, instruct, and convict His disciples of both sin and righteousness. Instead teens are confronted with the external expectations of those around them. Many, for a season, seek to live up to these external expectations hoping to see real change in their lives, only to be disappointed later. Our young people have not been taught to listen to the voice of the Helper. They have been trained to listen to the voice of men, which by itself, is devoid of the power to bring about deep life change.

Our teens do not understand that the Holy Spirit plays a vital role in the sanctification process, in the transformation of their lives to become more Christ-like. Previously we discussed how young people often believe that knowledge is the convicting agent of God, yet we see Jesus clearly teaching that the Holy Spirit convicts the world of sin and righteousness. Our youth desperately need to understand who the Holy Spirit is and what He can accomplish in their lives.

It seems in our quest to protect kids from the mistakes and harm that can come to them through parties, drugs, sex, and pornography, we take upon ourselves the role of the Holy Spirit. We try to sanctify them through our own efforts before they leave our homes. This is an impossible goal since sanctification is a life-long process. Our students aren't given the opportunity to develop sensitivity to the still quiet voice of conviction concerning sin and righteousness that flows from the Helper, the Holy Spirit. They are not prepared to listen to the voice of the Spirit when they leave our homes and ministries. Instead they have been trained to listen to the voice of mankind and they frequently find themselves listening to those that draw them away from the Lord.

In interacting with teens on this topic, the most common question is, "How do I know where the Holy Spirit is convicting or leading me?" That question once was foreign to me as well. Now it deeply saddens me. Romans 2:29 indicates that the Holy Spirit circumcises the heart of mankind. Our youth, who know much about God and the truth of right and wrong, need this deep transformation. Through our *Reboot* retreats we have found that when teens encounter the conviction and transformation of their hearts through the Spirit, it is life changing, especially for the postmodern who needs to experience the reality of truth to be sold out to it.

Because they are young and idealistic, youth perceive that they must implement everything they know right now, today. It's no wonder they feel like they are falling short a significant percentage of the time. This dampens their response to our teaching and the truth. We must help them come to understand how to follow the Holy Spirit's path for growth using the knowledge they have. As He brings issues to light, they will be free from the sense that reading Scripture will just show them more to do or not do. Instead they will be open to listening for the Spirit's next step in their individual sanctification process as they read their Bibles.

Jesus clearly sought to shift the dependence of His disciples from being on Him to being on the Spirit who would go with the disciples wherever they went. As leaders and parents we too need to point teens to the Spirit who can strengthen, guide, remind, and convict them beyond our doors.

QUESTIONS AND REFLECTIONS

How do your sheep perceive your role in their lives?

Jesus repeatedly sent the message to the disciples that He would not always be with them. How are you communicating that message to your teen?

If you are sending similar messages, are they being perceived in the same ways the disciples perceived the message from Jesus?

How does your approach to your teen recognize the life-long sanctification process the Holy Spirit is working out in all of us?

How can you begin to turn the leadership of your teen's life over to the Holy Spirit today?

Reflection

Recently one of our daughters was caught cheating on a test. My wife had a choice to make when she was handed the letter—handle this with a stern voice of conviction or something different. She asked, "How do you feel about this?" Our daughter answered, "Horrible!" Discussing it later in private, our daughter expressed that she felt horrible because she felt guilty. The Holy Spirit was doing His job. Continuing the discussion my wife asked if she knew how to deal with the guilty feeling. Our 10-year-old said no. After explaining how to walk in the light and confess wrongs to God, my wife asked if she wanted to pray. Yes, she did. After confessing, my wife asked, "Who else do you need to walk in the light with?" She knew it was her teacher. She decided on her own to write a letter and delivered it the next day. We didn't need to implement consequences because she had chosen to walk in the light and we wanted to encourage her to do so in the future.

CHAPTER TEN

WHEN THEY GRADUATE

*L*ori hated the thought of leaving her youth group. By her own account her youth group had been her family for the past four years. As she packed for college and later boarded the plane with her mom to travel from Georgia to Arizona, she realized for the first time how big of a change she was about to undertake. She had been so busy with school, work, friends, and church through her final semester of high school, she was able to deny the coming change. Now, sitting on the plane preparing to take off, it struck her that she knew virtually no one on campus except for one guy she had met earlier that year.

Lori's sense of discomfort grew when she arrived at Northern Arizona University and moved into the freshman dorm. She knew absolutely no one in a building that held 1,000 students. A day later after locating the cafeteria, the bookstore and her class buildings, she drove her mom to the airport and said good-bye. Her loneliness and sense of being out of place were unbearable as she drove slowly back to campus. She was stressed from having a stranger for a roommate and harbored a feeling of overwhelming loneliness. She literally felt sick. On top of her anxiety she faced the unknown responsibilities of life on her own without a plan for success socially, financially, or academically. She had stepped into an entirely different culture, unprepared and unconnected.

As Lori sat in her dorm room that afternoon she heard people talking about going to a party that evening. Several asked her if she *wanted to go and of course she said yes. She didn't want to sit in her room, alone, fighting back tears of loneliness on the first night on campus. That evening, without realizing it, she set the course for her entire freshman year.*

Now at a party in just her second night on campus, she was compelled to escape the uneasy feelings she had regarding her place in this new world. Her God-given needs to be loved and accepted were spiking through the roof in a way she had never before encountered. No one had even tried to warn her about the dangers of stress and loneliness and how they could open one to bonding to foreign cultures in a short period of time. Lori was simply carried along by the intense emotions lying deep within.

She describes her first days like this: "I remember very little of that first week on campus because I pretty much drank it all away." In her third day on campus she moved out of her freshman dorm into sorority housing hoping to find a community to replace all she was missing from home. She was surrounded by upper classman who were throwing parties to attract new recruits. She had bonded to the party culture in her first seventy-two hours on campus!

When classes began the following week, her loneliness began to decrease but the stress of life on her own and the attached responsibilities increased. Lori needed to watch her money because she was on a scholarship and needed a job. The pressure of finances, school, and the social culture led to a regular lifestyle of parties. They helped her escape the pressure and sense of displacement from being at the opposite end of the country from her mom and friends. Facebook could not replace her need for friends who she could be with on campus and in person.

Lori was a victim. She was unprepared for the changes, loneliness, and stress that accompany major life events. Unfortunately she also ended up a victim of sexual assault at a party during her first semester of college. Seven years later the ramifications of her bonding to the party scene are still being played out in her life.

- Did Lori set out to leave the faith when she left home? No.
- Did she intend to find a church or a ministry when she arrived? Yes.
- Did she know the name of any of the college ministries before leaving home? No.
- Was she involved in a ministry in her first year at NAU? No.
- Did her mom drop her off and pray that she would be OK? Yes, every night.
- Was she OK?

Today, as shepherds of young people, it seems that we tend to forfeit the game in the last two minutes. This is done unintentionally because we believe we've done all we can. We believe it's time for our young people to stand on their own two feet, which is both true and false.

Research from Ohio State University shows that a vast majority of students who leave home have done little or nothing to prepare for the changes and responsibilities they will face in college.[20] Parents may assume this preparation has been handled at school and schools may believe it is occurring at home, but the fact remains that little preparation occurs.

Compounding this, students believe the transition from home will be easy because they are so looking forward to being done with high school. As a result, they do not forecast the stress, loneliness, and challenges.

Research tells the story; 26 percent of all college freshmen do not make it through their first year of college. The research states three of the top contributors to this failure:

1. Changes in the social environment
2. Changes in the academic protocol
3. Managing time

In addition to these, students are on their own spiritually for the first time in their lives. This creates the perfect storm!

Research done by Fuller Seminary's Youth Institute into the transition of youth group graduates to college confirms the Ohio State findings that social change is the number one difficulty for youth group graduates. The top three difficulties according to Fuller Theological Seminary for youth in transition are:[21]

1. Aloneness
2. Making friends
3. A desire to find a church but not knowing how

As a result of loneliness and lack of connection to a ministry, the study also revealed that 100 percent of the youth group graduates tracked had used alcohol and 69 percent had a sexual encounter in their first year on campus.

Culture Shock

The combination of change, responsibility, and loneliness leads to an incredible level of stress which can create a physiological response known as culture shock. Culture shock has been studied by mission agencies for some time and is actually used to help missionaries cast off the presuppositions of their culture so that they can bond and be effective in a foreign culture. The military uses culture shock to take some of our wildest teens and bond them to an entirely authoritarian culture in just a few short weeks.

In many ways culture shock is what our teens face as they leave home. Change, increased responsibility, and loneliness result in a level of stress that they have never before encountered. Dr. Steven Bochner defines the stress that creates culture shock like this:

Stress is a force brought on by uncertainty and change which creates upset stomachs, gnawing fear, headaches, intense grief, excessive drinking and arguments. Stress dulls our memory, weakens our bodies, stirs up our emotions and reduces efficiency.[22]

This definition mirrors Lori's experience during her first week at NAU. In that week she encountered fear, stomachaches, and intense grief, though she did not recognize it. She drank excessively, not even remembering how she got to several of the parties. Her immune system was compromised and she came down with strep throat but did not go to the doctor the first week. Instead she kept on partying to escape the tangled feelings she was experiencing as she desperately sought a place to fit in.

This level of stress leads to culture shock which acts upon people in this fashion:

Often individuals in a contact situation will, when the second culture has higher status then their own, reject the culture of their origin and adopt the new culture.[23]

Living in a dorm is a high contact situation where students are immersed in a new culture that has a much higher perceived status than being in high school and living at home. These quotes can be found in *Culture Shock* which is a book on missions. They support our video interviews with college freshmen that indicate that the forces acting upon them are in every way consistent with culture shock.

Because of the dangers present on college campuses, some parents have decided that keeping their kids at home and sending them to community college is a safer alternative. Our interviews with community college students, while not conclusive, call this strategy into question. These students tend to be the loneliest students we meet in spite of being at home.

While living at home with their parents, their relational needs go unmet and tension often increases with parents because they feel like they should be on their own. Compounding this is the fact that there is little community on many community college campuses. To some students it seems like a glorified high school where everyone has different schedules. The students are on and off campus as fast as possible because there is little social networking. In addition, staying at home usually means attending the same church where they no longer fit in the youth group. Only one in fifteen churches has something for the age group following high school. In all likelihood, college students will not be connected to a viable community at their church. Finally, because community colleges largely lack the infrastructure that encourages student gathering and community, very few have viable college ministries available.

One of the Youth Transition Network's board members believed that community college was the best course for his daughter. She was their first high school graduate. The results in her life were devastating even though she was still at home. After learning more from the Youth Transition Network and understanding the dynamics of the college transition event, he was better prepared. His son attended a four-year university and was connected to a ministry before leaving home. His freshmen year on a secular campus was nothing but positive and he grew closer to God!

It is vital that parents of postmodern students, who value community more than almost anything else, truly explore and assess the community their students will experience.

There is no perfect answer to the choice of a college. All have strengths and weaknesses. The topic of the transition and of choosing a college will be more thoroughly discussed in a forthcoming book, *Before They Graduate*. Here is a brief summary of the options.

Community College

There is little community and often no college ministry. As a result, students tend to be the loneliest and typically have to pursue relationships outside of the college through their work.[24]

Secular College or University

A vibrant community typically exists, unless it is a commuter college or university like Arizona State University which has a high percentage of students who commute. Temptation is high; but there are typically multiple college ministries available to help students navigate college and their faith on a secular campus. Use LiveAbove.com to identify the ministries available on every campus in the country. Your graduate can use this site to connect with these ministries before they leave home.

Christian College

There is a vibrant community. Students are surrounded by Christian faculty and have required Bible classes and chapel. But the dual life found in youth groups is often quite prevalent on the Christian college campus as well. Students will have access to all that is available on a secular campus; it is just more hidden.

Our students today need community more than ever. While technology makes this generation the most connected in history, research also indicates they are the loneliest generation ever. This explains why their need for community is so high and why, as parents, the relationship we have with our students is so vital.

The friends and community our graduates make in the first few days on a college campus will in a large part set the course for their life in college. Thinking through the types of communities available, knowing the status of your students' life and faith, and determining what will encourage or discourage their faith are vital to making a good college selection today.

Does the fact that friends and community influence our students mean their faith is weak? Not necessarily. The strength of their individual faith alone does not determine the outcome. Culture shock and the drive for community are powerful forces that can distract our students and pull many away from the Lord.

Life's Stressors

We have all seen life stress tests with which we can calculate the total stress points in our lives. Some of the events with the highest point ratings are moving, a death in the family, and a job change.

If we look at the transition to life on their own through a student's eyes we find that:

- They have moved.
- Their family experience has died.
- They have a new job in college with a syllabus and totally different expectations.
- They may also need to find a new paying job.

Life stress tests would put the point total for these activities in the nervous breakdown range! It seems that often in the church we want to look only at spiritual issues and solutions. When we go to do missions or inner city work, we look to meet practical needs and issues. We often overlook the ardently practical needs of our youth. We sidestep a holistic approach to youth ministry that addresses practical needs that could help more juniors and seniors continue in their faith and our ministries.

Preparing students for the stress, responsibilities, and changes helps them accurately read their new surroundings and the feelings buffeting them in those first weeks on campus. Helping them be aware of these forces also increases their desire to find a Christian community before arriving on campus.

The topics we need to address with our students include:

- Loneliness
- Stress
- Making new friends
- Living with roommates
- The value of a sound community

- Managing time and setting priorities in an unstructured day
- Managing finances on campus

When students have an understanding of the reality of the changes they will face and have some idea of where and what they will do to address them on their own, their fear and stress levels are greatly reduced when they arrive on campus. They will be less vulnerable to the temptations and emotional forces that can be so powerful regardless of their faith.

Preparing our graduates is like having a good two-minute offense in football. At the end of the game they have a pre-established plan and the effort and intensity increases. We need to have this mindset with our high school juniors and seniors. Our job is not done with the SAT and ACT prep courses, the college application, the acceptance letter, or even the housing forms and tuition. It is done once our students have a game plan to tackle the change, stress, and responsibilities of the first days, weeks, and semester on campus. Visit our website, YouthTransitionNetwork. org to find resources that will help move your students past the denial that the change will be difficult and for resources to help them prepare for their future.

PRIORITIES

The loss of youth is a multifaceted issue with no magic bullets. No one group, parents, youth leaders, senior pastors, or teens can individually address the full range of contributing causes in the life of even a single student. To address the various issues at hand will require each group to seek to shepherd our young people. Leaders and parents are pulled in so many directions that setting priorities is essential. Will we collectively place a high enough priority on this issue to bring about change that will make a difference? What priority will we as families, churches, youth leaders, and senior pastors place upon our young people in the midst of all the other important things the body of Christ needs to address? Do we truly believe that our youth represent the future of the church and its ability to carry out local and global missions?

In our churches today, we allocate resources for the youth ministry to outreach and engage our young people. But where is the true priority within our churches overall? More importantly, have we specifically and deliberately defined our youth ministry's purpose? Is it to:

- Attract every student who attends church?
- Bring new families into our church?
- Reach the unsaved in our high schools?

- Make disciples?
- Develop the next generation of church leadership?

What are our priorities and objectives for our young people? We must wrestle with these questions given that the average youth pastor is often working with three to four different groups of parents who all want different things from the youth group. The church may have a senior pastor who once was a youth pastor and who thinks in terms of that experience. Finally, the church leadership is often lobbied by the different views. In essence the tire is out of balance because we are not unified concerning the purpose and desired outcomes of our youth ministries. This places the youth pastor in the position of doing what has always been done, but hopefully better than the last guy because moving out in a different direction may bring opposition from one or more sides.

Often what is lost is the Good Shepherd's call to care for the well-being of His flock. Clearly Jesus wanted to reach the unsaved; but what was His top priority? One thing is evident; if we want to reverse the loss of youth, we must first make them a top priority.

Ministry Focus

As we consider priorities I'm struck by how great our focus is upon evangelism and outreach. In many ministries this seems to be driven by the fact that not very much outreach is actually occurring. As we interact with para-church ministries across the country we find that the primary focus is on the unsaved, because working with church kids is seen as difficult and a distraction from the mission of evangelism.

Yet every year we watch roughly 673,000 of our young people walk away from the body of Christ as they move beyond high school graduation. During the 2008-2009 school year on college campuses across the country, the decisions for Christ in the annual reports of our college ministries were less than 20,000 when combined! We lose 673,000 and add 20,000 new on-fire converts. How many businesses would give up 673,000 current customers to get 20,000 new ones? This is a matter of priority. Donors fund ministries and donors are far more motivated by evangelism than maintaining the flock. This leads to the types of ministries that exist today. The realization of the loss and our current focus indicate that we should examine the priorities of the Good Shepherd.

Redefining Lost

Today we often use the word *lost* solely to describe the unsaved. Obviously, we place a high priority upon reaching them. As I speak with youth who have left the church, they too appear to be lost as they are no longer connected to the church or the Lord. They venture out into the world for the first time without a shepherd.

Reflecting on Jesus and His statement that "no one can snatch them out of My hand" raises questions like:

- What would Jesus do in our situation?
- Who was at the top of Jesus' priority list?
- Whom did Jesus view as lost?

Looking at Jesus' teaching, it appears that He did not consider everyone to be part of His flock. In John 10:25-27, He says

> I told you, and you do not believe; the works that I do in My Father's name, these bear witness of Me. But you do not believe because **you are not of My sheep**. My sheep hear My voice, and I know them, and they follow Me (emphasis added).

According to Jesus, His sheep are those who hear His voice and follow it, as the disciples did. Those who did not listen and understand were not His sheep.

Having been on staff with Campus Crusade for Christ and having shared my faith on campus, on the beach, at the Boulder Mall, and many other places, I understood my mission to be reaching the lost with the gospel. As a result, when I met with church graduates the first week on campus who were not excited to become involved, or ready to serve and reach out, I did not see them as part of my mission. In that context I missed connecting with many overwhelmed students who were stressed and were avoiding more commitments. I did not see them as lost sheep. To this day I believe I will face accountability for the many sheep I walked past in my years on campus. In John 10:27-28 we find Jesus saying:

> My sheep hear My voice, and I know them, and they follow Me; and I give eternal life to them, and they will never perish; and **no one will snatch them out of My hand** (emphasis added).

Clearly this passage applies to believers and not unbelievers. Believers cannot be snatched from His hand, indicating a strong commitment and priority upon His flock of believers.

In Matthew 18:12-14 Jesus teaches about leaving ninety-nine sheep on the mountainside to go after one lost sheep.

> What do you think? If any man has a hundred sheep, and one of them has gone astray, does he not leave the ninety-nine on the mountains and go and search for the one that is straying? And if it turns out that he finds it, truly I say to you, he rejoices over it more than over the ninety-nine, which have not gone astray. Thus it is not the will of your Father who is in heaven that one of these little ones perish.

It is not immediately obvious from this passage if Jesus views the flock as everyone in the world or as only those from His flock. Looking at the context and audience takes us back to Matthew 18:1-6, where Jesus is talking about the little ones.

*At that time the disciples came to Jesus and said, "Who is the greatest in the kingdom of heaven?" And He called a child to Himself and set him before them, and said, "Truly I say to you, unless you are converted and become like children, you will not enter the kingdom of heaven. Whoever then humbles himself as this child, he is the greatest in the kingdom of heaven. And whoever receives one such child in My name receives Me; but whoever causes one of these little ones **who believe in Me** to stumble, it would be better for him that a heavy millstone be hung around his neck, and that he be drowned in the depth of the sea (emphasis added).*

This passage describes how valuable Jesus views the little ones of the faith. He stresses this by emphasizing how serious it is to cause one of them to stumble. Just imagine tying a 180-pound millstone around your neck and jumping into deep water! We also discover that these little ones are the little ones "who believe in Me," church kids who have accepted Christ at a young age. Many want to debate whether they are truly believers. This passage would indicate that Jesus honors the faith decisions of children and that He places a high priority on the little ones who believe in Him!

Looking back at the ninety-nine and the one, we find that the immediate context of Mathew18:12-14 is surrounded by references to the little ones.

Matthew 18:10:

See that you do not despise one of these little ones, for I say to you, that their angels in heaven continually behold the face of My Father who is in heaven.

Matthew 18:14:

Thus it is not the will of your Father who is in heaven that one of these little ones perish.

Given the whole passage and the immediate proximity to His teaching about the ninety-nine and the one lost sheep, Jesus viewed the one lost sheep as a believer ... one who was part of His flock, not one who was unsaved. Jesus used the word lost for a believer who had strayed!

We learn several things from the passage. First, while Jesus used the analogy of sheep for people. We are not sheep, but rather disciples. Unlike sheep we should be able to be left together on the hill without the shepherd for a period of time, capable of looking out for one another. This allows the Good Shepherd to pursue the one who has strayed. Second, there is great rejoicing when the lost believer is found and returned to the flock. Third, there is a very high value placed upon each member of Jesus' flock and a higher priority placed on those who stray from the flock.

Matthew 18:13

> *If it turns out that he finds it, truly I say to you, he rejoices over it more than over the ninety-nine which have not gone astray.*

The fact that 673,000 go astray each year with virtually no resources targeted at going after them should give us all a reason to pause, assess, pray, and envision what a priority on the lost sheep from our flock should look like.

Jesus took special care to set His disciples up to succeed once He returned to the Father. He was not willing that any should be lost. Let's ask ourselves: "Are we doing the same?" Given the magnitude of the loss we may also need to ask, "Are we actually causing our little ones to stumble?" If so, we need to diligently work to alter those things that impede the development of our young people into disciples and followers of Christ.

Measuring success

One of the ways to begin altering our course is by determining how we will measure success going forward. In our travels we have found that very few churches track the fruit of their youth ministry. Should we use the number attending every week, the number in small groups, the number who go on mission trips, or the number who are still walking with God a year after high school graduation?

It appears that Jesus based His measurement upon the disciples' faithfulness after His departure. Therefore it makes sense that the success of youth ministry would best be measured one-year after high school graduation. That measure should look at the percentage of all the graduates in the church who are still walking with God, not just a percentage of those who stayed involved in their youth group through their senior year. Measuring youth ministry in this fashion would lend itself toward ownership of all the youth in the church and require changes from year to year to encourage more and more students to continue through their senior year and beyond graduation.

One thing that struck me during the past five years is the general lack of concern with the back door of our churches. We are motivated by evangelism and even marketing to get new people in the front door of our churches and ministries, but little energy and few resources go into understanding or helping those who leave the church. It is clear that as shepherds we need to diligently pursue those who have gone astray from our flocks, not just let them wander off thinking they are now someone else's responsibility. As good shepherds we must first identify what is ailing our flock, and second, make sure they are connected to another flock before we release our responsibility for them.

The Good Shepherd said, "I lay down my life for my sheep" and "No one can snatch them out of my hand." If we are to be Christ-like, we too must take seriously not losing any of our own flock. We must invest the time to understand why our sheep are leaving, what we can do to avert the loss, and how we can pursue those who have gone astray.

There are many things we can begin to do today.

- Assess the view we have of young people, positive or negative.
- Evaluate the approach we take in teaching our young people (expectation or belief and trust).
- Determine the purpose of our youth ministry.
- Decide how our youth ministry success is measured.
- Alter the way we as parents lead/shepherd our pre-teens and teens.
- Examine what we will do to prepare and shepherd our young people in transition.
- Plan to address the practical needs of our graduates.
- Prioritize going after those that stray from our flock.

In setting priorities around such things we can truly begin to avert the phenomena of going, going, gone in the hearts and minds of our young people as they move toward life on their own. We need to have the same mentality Jesus had toward His disciples as He looked ahead to His departure and prepared them to succeed on their own! We must not let anyone or anything snatch them out of our hands!

Questions and Reflections

What practical needs do juniors and seniors in high school have that we can meet?

What is our game plan to help insure a successful transition beyond high school graduation?

How will we continue to show love and care for our sheep after graduation in order to keep the lines of communication open?

Reflection

Jesus was the Good Shepherd. In the face of His disciple's failure upon His arrest, Jesus returned dispensing grace, choosing not to deliver a message of condemnation or weak faith. Instead, He put them back in the game by encouraging them and issuing them the Great Commission. Although in Hebrews 10:24 the Bible says, "stimulate each other onto love and good deeds," our human nature bends us toward a model based upon "convicting each other onto love and good deeds."

ENDNOTES

1. "Church Dropouts: How many leave the church between ages 18 and 22 and why?" *LifeWayResearch.com* LifeWay, April 2007.

2. National Center for Education Statistics, *nces.ed.gov*. There are 2.8 million public school graduates and 300,000 private school graduates annually according to NCES.

3. Barna Group. "Twentysomethings Struggle to Find Their Place in Christian Churches." *Barna.org* N.p., 24 Sep. 2003.

4. "First Year of College is the Riskiest." *USA Today* 25 Jan. 2006: 1. Print.

5. "Church Dropouts: How many leave the church between ages 18 and 22 and why?" *LifeWayResearch.com* LifeWay, April 2007.

6. 3.1 million students graduate every year according to NCES. Thirty-one percent of them attend church regularly according to Barna Group. This equates to 961,000 ministry graduates annually. Based upon LifeWay research 70 percent will take a break from church or 673,000. If 35 percent return by age thirty 236,000 will return on an annual basis. The result is that 438,000 people have not returned to the church by age thirty.

7. Barna Group. "New Marriage and Divorce Statistics Released." *Barna.org* N.p., 31 Mar. 2008.

8. "Hope." *Encarta World English Dictionary.* Microsoft Corporation, N.p., 1999. All rights reserved. Developed for Microsoft by Bloomsbury Publishing Plc.

9. Raison, Brian. "Study Identifies Areas Where Pre-College Programming Needed." *E-Source Journal,* National Center for First-Year Experience & Students in Transition 5.6 (2008). Print.

10. "Listening to Students about Leaving the Church." *YTN Newsletter* 8 (2007):1.

11. This is an excellent question for any youth pastor to ask their students. Please be prayerful about asking it first; then be prepared for the potential responses.

12. The full list of expectations can be viewed under the research section at YouthTransitionNetwork.org.

13. Center for Parent Youth Understanding (2009) About CPYU, Retrieved August 23, 2008 from *cpyu.org.*

14. "Expectation." *Encarta World English Dictionary.* Microsoft Corporation, N.p., 1999. All rights reserved. Developed for Microsoft by Bloomsbury Publishing Plc.

15. "Lead." *Encarta World English Dictionary.* Microsoft Corporation, N.p., 1999. All rights reserved. Developed for Microsoft by Bloomsbury Publishing Plc.

16. "Leader." *Encarta World English Dictionary.* Microsoft Corporation, N.p., 1999. All rights reserved. Developed for Microsoft by Bloomsbury Publishing Plc.

17. "Shepherd." *Encarta World English Dictionary.* Microsoft Corporation, N.p., 1999. All rights reserved. Developed for Microsoft by Bloomsbury Publishing Plc.

18. In Hebrews chapter 11 the author discusses many men and women who have gone before us who by faith accomplished great things for God.

19. "Christian Endeavor." *Wikipedia: The Free Encyclopedia* N.p. Web. 18 Jan. 2010. Christian Endeavor was founded by Francis Edward Clark in 1881 and by 1908 it had 70,000 chapters in the U.S. and 3.5 million members.

20. Raison, Brain. "College 101: Strategies for First Year

Success—A Program for High School Seniors." Journal of Youth Development Mar (2007). Print.

21. Fuller Theological Seminary's Center for Youth & Family Ministry. College Transition Project, pilot phase, January 2005.

22. Bochner, Stephen. *Psychology of Culture Shock.* (Philadelphia: Taylor & Francis Inc., 1986.) Print.

23. Bochner, Stephen. *Psychology of Culture Shock.* (Philadelphia: Taylor & Francis Inc., 1986.) Print.

24. Youth Transition Network video interviews, 2006-2009. Based upon video interviews with over three hundred college students.

A powerful DVD containing 8 video segments with candid college student stories about their transition, which gives your students a look into the social, academic, financial, and spiritual realities of life beyond high school helping to motivate them to connect with a community of believers before leaving home. View the video content online at http://videoroom.YTN.org.

This highly interactive hour and a half session is designed for you to present to your high school juniors and seniors. The session incorporates Biblical content and a professionally designed Power Point with embedded college student video clips to prepare your graduates for the stress, loneliness, and temptation they will face when they leave home. Visit YTN.org/resources to learn more.

An 8 session video series designed to set your high school graduate up to succeed beyond high school. Succeed 2010 incorporates college student stories, dynamic speakers, a college student panel with discussion questions after each session helping to prepare your high school graduate for the social, academic, financial, worldview, and spiritual realities they will face after high school. Succeed on DVD can be used by a family to prepare their graduate helping to facilitate discussions around challenging topics or in a youth group with juniors and seniors preparing to go to a community, Christian, or four-year college. Visit YTN.org/resources to order today!

This challenging seminar series and soon-to-be book is designed to help parents of pre-teens and teens counteract the impact our society has upon our developing young adults. Based upon research conducted with 1,500 teens the series incorporates high school student videos, research results, and a deep look into the approach Jesus took with his band of disciples to set them up to succeed beyond His time among them. As parents we all want to see our students do well beyond our front door yet the very things we believe will help them grow up to be responsible, healthy young adults may be driving them away from us and their faith! Learn more about bringing a Shepherding for the Future Seminar to your church or city by calling 602-441-2240 x 104 or visiting YTN.org today.

COMING SOON
Before They Graduate **by Jeff Schadt**
Every parent wants their high school graduate to succeed beyond their front door. This book is filled with actual stories and practical tips from research conducted with 500 college students. It will help you better understand your teen and the reasons so many struggle when they leave home. *Before They Graduate* addresses topics like: preparing them for the change, selecting the best collegiate option for your child, and motivating and connecting them to a body of believers before they leave home. If your high school student is headed toward college—whether secular, Christian, or a community college this book will help you guide your graduate towards success academically, financially, socially, and spiritually.

To Review More Research and Blog with the author, go to
www.GoingGoingGone.com

Jeff Schadt